Timesaver London!

(Elementary – Intermediate)

Sarah Johnson
and Jane Myles

SCHOLASTIC

MARY GLASGOW MAGAZINES

Contents

Elementary *(Students with up to 1 year of English)*

Pre-intermediate *(Students with 1-2 years of English)*

Intermediate *(Students with 2-3 years of English)*

Teacher's Notes and Background Information

Key to symbols:

Elementary
(students with up to 1 year of English)

Pre-intermediate
(students with 1-2 years of English)

Intermediate
(students with 2-3 years of English)

The clock symbol at the top of each new topic indicates approximately how many minutes the reading section and extension activity should take.

Most of the pages in this book will need no further explanation. The elementary pages contain interactive sections of text alongside short reading passages. In the later pre-intermediate and intermediate pages, there is usually a reading page on the left and an exploitation page on the right-hand side, but occasionally a one-page topic which contains combined factual text and an integrated exercise.

The levels

The language used in the book extends from elementary level through to intermediate. In some cases, the grammatical structures will be simple, but the vocabulary may be a bit more obscure which is why you may find a page classified under pre-intermediate rather than elementary level.

Follow-up projects

Where possible we have included website addresses so that you can do further research. However, as always, please be warned that although the sites were checked before going to press, the nature of websites and their content can change or the entire site may become inactive.

The vocabulary check lists

You will notice that there are short vocabulary check lists accompanying each topic. We suggest that before you begin a topic, you photocopy the word check list or copy it onto the board to see if students can predict what they think the topic is going to be. Take a vote to see what the majority of students think it is. If there are several different suggestions, see if the students representing one opinion can persuade others from a different group by giving reasons for certain words being in the list. At this stage they don't have to translate all the words in the list. The meanings of some of the words will be deduced from their context in the reading passage.

You can allocate one word from the check list to each student in advance of the lesson, and then get them to explain to the rest of the class what it means and how it is pronounced.

Using the map

On pages 6 & 7 you will find a rough map of London which tries to include as many of the locations mentioned in this book as possible. Those which are too far from the centre are indicated with directional arrows.

Using the key to the map (*on page 5*), you can practise numbers as well as teaching your students a lot of basic London geography.

Ask, for example:
Can you see number 4 on the map?
Which other numbers are near it? (5 and 6)
Which two places/numbers is it between?
Students can then guess what they think it might be.

Alternatively, you could ask:
What number do you think the Tower of London is?
and see how many students get it right.

You can enlarge the map on a photocopier and this will then give students a bit more space to write in the names of the places next to the numbers if you call them out as a dictation exercise.

As further extension work, get students to work with actual maps of London and see what other landmarks they can identify and add to their own photocopied maps, eg *10, Downing Street, the home of the Prime Minister, Covent Garden, Baker Street*, or *Waterloo Station.*

Once you have done quite a lot of pages from the book, you could ask students to look at their copies of the map and ask people to talk for a few minutes about 'number...' on the map, since they will have learned quite a lot of facts by doing the activities in this book, eg, *Anna, can you talk for five minutes about number 3?*

If the nominated student is struggling to remember or to put their thoughts into English, you can ask for other volunteers to help them out.

1	Heathrow Airport	19	Oxford Street
2	The London Eye	20	Chinatown
3	The Tower of London	21	Wimbledon
		22	Battersea
4	Big Ben	23	London Aquarium
5	Houses of Parliament	24	London Zoo
6	Westminster Abbey	25	Regent's Park
7	The Natural History Museum	26	Hyde Park
		27	Richmond Park
8	Madame Tussaud's	28	St Paul's Cathedral
9	Buckingham Palace	29	Notting Hill
10	Tate Modern	30	The British Museum
11	Tate Britain	31	Hampton Court
12	The National Gallery	32	The London Dungeon
13	Trafalgar Square		
14	Hamleys	33	The Science Museum
15	Harrods	34	Greenwich
16	Portobello Road	35	Royal Albert Hall
17	Piccadilly Circus	36	Festival Hall
18	Leicester Square	37	HMS Belfast

Background information

History

The history of London as a permanent settlement stretches back almost two thousand years. The city has no known founder. Shortly after the Roman conquest of 43 AD, the invaders grasped the strategic significance of the River Thames, slicing through the flattest, most fertile portion of their new province, its estuary providing easy access to the European mainland. Londinium, as it was then known, became a thriving city.

With the collapse of Roman administration, Londinium was abandoned in the fifth century. The invading Anglo-Saxons were farmers who gradually pushed the native Romano-British westwards. They had no taste for city life and preferred to found villages which are now London's suburbs or satellites such as Fulham, Mitcham, Ealing and Barking.

The Norman invasion of 1066 was marked by the construction of the Tower of London, which protected London Bridge from raiders coming upstream and was built to overawe its inhabitants as a symbol and embodiment of royal power.

London was devastated by the epidemic of bubonic plague, known as the Black Death, which carried off a third of the population in 1348-9.

The population of London tripled under the Tudors, making it the greatest city in Britain – almost a hundred times more populous than the Stratford-on-Avon in which Shakespeare grew up before coming to the Globe Theatre as actor-manager. Two devastating events took place during the reign of Charles II – the Great Plague in 1665, and the Great Fire of London which destroyed many of the city's most beautiful buildings a year later in 1666. Although half the city was destroyed, only six people were injured.

By 1700, London's population had passed the half-million mark, ranking it with Paris and Naples as one of Europe's three largest cities. However, with the Industrial Revolution in the nineteenth century, squalor and poverty accompanied its rapid growth. Charles Dickens chronicled much of this in his novels.

When Edward VII ascended the throne in 1901, London was the largest city in the world, with a population of over six million. A century later it is still the largest city in Europe.

Facts and figures

Population: 7.19 million. This means that one in eight of the UK population live in London. 47% of these people are aged 16 to 44 and one in four of London's population is from an ethnic minority.

Language: Over 200 languages are spoken in London. London is a global centre for international business with over 25% of the world's largest companies having their European headquarters in London

Parks: Almost a third of London is green space or parks (many of which are Royal Parks) – more than any other city of its size in the world.

Transport: There are 20,000 licensed taxis in London, 20,000 buses and 275 underground stations.

Food and drink: There are 6,000 restaurants and 5,000 pubs and bars. The restaurants serve food from seventy different countries.

Historic buildings: London has 151 historic buildings and ancient monuments and 33 historic gardens. There are over 18,000 historically listed buildings in London, nearly 600 of which are Grade I listed (ie extremely important) and 21% of which are within the borough of Westminster. There are three world heritage sites in London: the Tower of London, Maritime Greenwich and Westminster Abbey.

Entertainment: London has over 200 museums, 500 cinema screens and 108 theatres and music halls. There are 1,500 drama groups, 600 dance groups and five symphony orchestras.

Sport: 95 golf courses, 50 athletics tracks, 2000 tennis courts, seven ice rinks, 546 swimming pools, 37 rowing clubs, 12 professional football teams, two county cricket clubs and six race courses all within an hour of London.

Tourism: In 2002, 28 million people visited for at least one night.

This is London

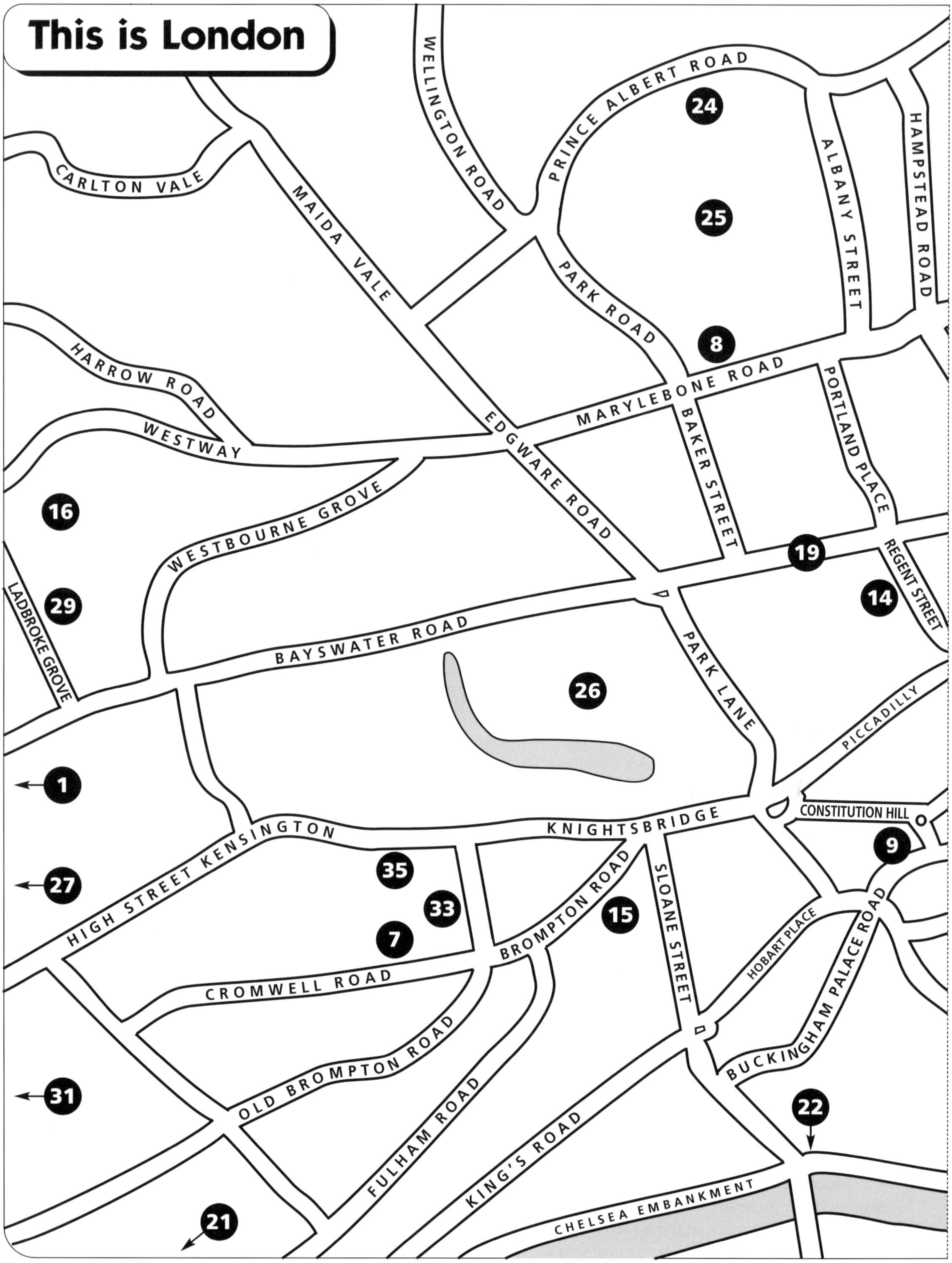

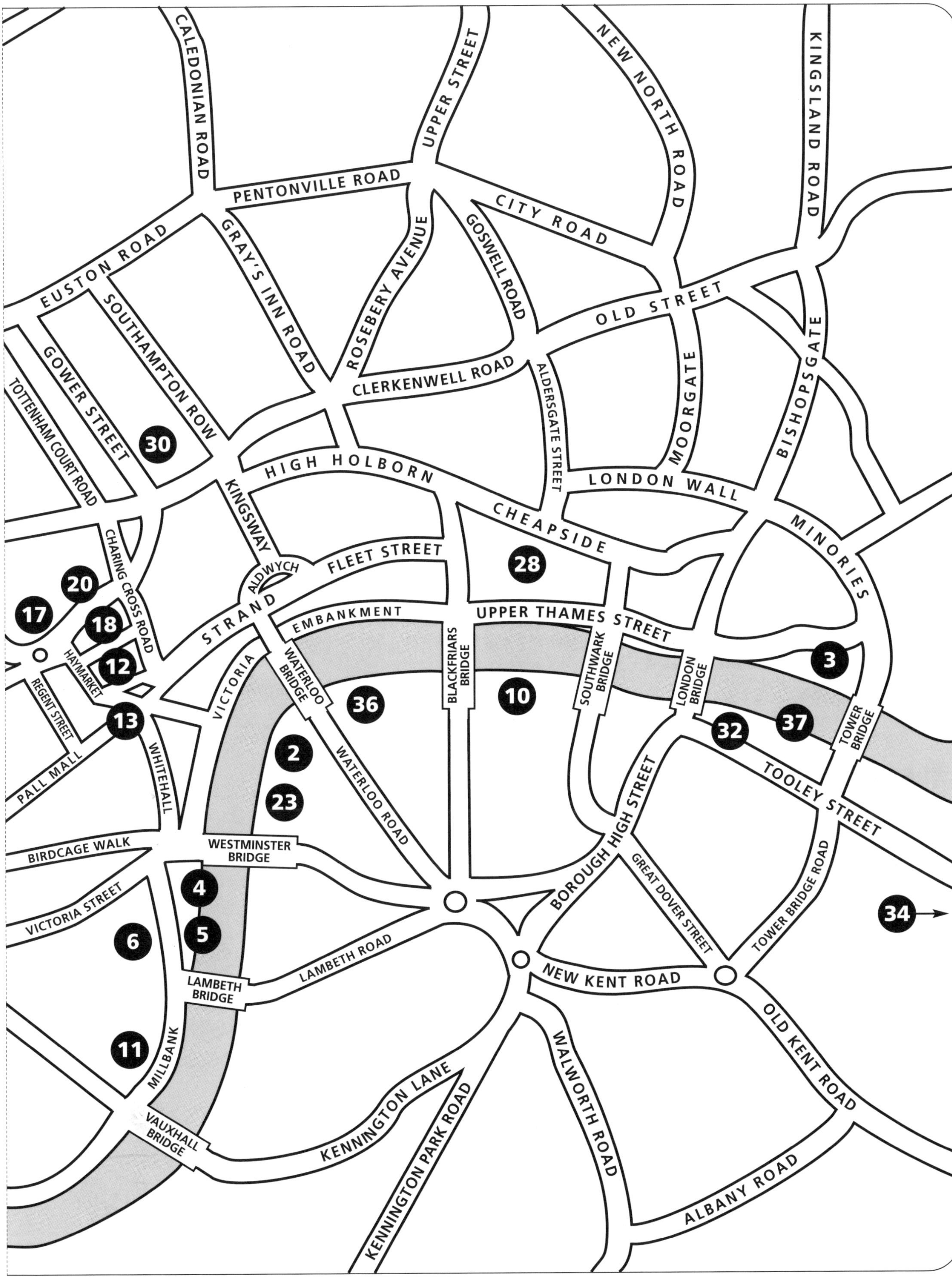
CALEDONIAN ROAD
UPPER STREET
NEW NORTH ROAD
KINGSLAND ROAD
PENTONVILLE ROAD
CITY ROAD
EUSTON ROAD
GRAY'S INN ROAD
ROSEBERY AVENUE
GOSWELL ROAD
OLD STREET
SOUTHAMPTON ROW
GOWER STREET
TOTTENHAM COURT ROAD
CLERKENWELL ROAD
ALDERSGATE STREET
MOORGATE
BISHOPSGATE
30
HIGH HOLBORN
LONDON WALL
KINGSWAY
CHEAPSIDE
MINORIES
CHARING CROSS ROAD
FLEET STREET
28
ALDWYCH
20
17
18
STRAND
EMBANKMENT
UPPER THAMES STREET
HAYMARKET
12
VICTORIA
WATERLOO BRIDGE
BLACKFRIARS BRIDGE
SOUTHWARK BRIDGE
LONDON BRIDGE
3
REGENT STREET
36
10
13
32
37
TOWER BRIDGE
2
PALL MALL
WHITEHALL
WATERLOO ROAD
TOOLEY STREET
23
BOROUGH HIGH STREET
BIRDCAGE WALK
WESTMINSTER BRIDGE
4
GREAT DOVER STREET
TOWER BRIDGE ROAD
34
VICTORIA STREET
5
6
LAMBETH ROAD
NEW KENT ROAD
LAMBETH BRIDGE
OLD KENT ROAD
11
MILLBANK
WALWORTH ROAD
KENNINGTON LANE
KENNINGTON PARK ROAD
VAUXHALL BRIDGE
ALBANY ROAD

Arriving in London

Most people who come to London come by plane. There are five airports for London, but the most famous and popular are Heathrow and Gatwick.

1 Find the five airports and write the names in the correct places.

Heathrow: This is the busiest* airport in the world. It's west of London.

Gatwick: This airport is for many people going to holiday destinations*. It's south of London.

Stansted: This airport is good for cheap* flights. It's north-east of London.

Luton: This airport is in a town north of London. It's also a good airport for cheap flights.

City: This is a small airport near the city of London. It's for short flights and business flights.

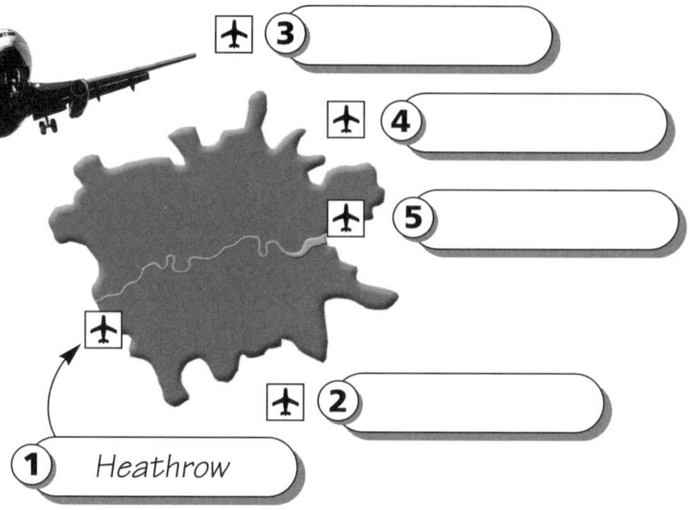

2 You land in London and get off* the plane. You see three signs*. Where do you go?

☐ Check-in ➤

☐ Passport control ➤

☐ Departures ➤

A British passport looks like this. Now fill in a passport for yourself.

Photo	Name: ______
	Date of Birth: ______
	Place of Birth: ______
	Passport Number: ______

3 Now you need to find your bags and suitcases. Where do you go?

☐ Toilets ➤ ☐ Duty-free ➤ ☐ Baggage reclaim ➤

4 You are in the baggage hall. You arrive from Lisbon, Portugal. You have got a large rucksack and a large old suitcase. Where's your luggage?

Arrivals	Flight number	Time	Baggage reclaim number
Barcelona	BA 2549871	13:40	4
Warsaw	LOT 2377877	delayed	–
Berlin	LH 588910	13:45	1
Lisbon	BA 097177	14:00	3
Milan	ALIT 324417	14:05	6
Vienna	AUST 71928	delayed	–

5 **You want to leave the airport. Where do you go?**

☐ Gates 1–10 ➤ ☐ Exit ➤ ☐ Entrance ➤

To get to the centre of London from the airport is very easy. You can go by bus, train or taxi.

6 **Many visitors go to the centre of London by train. Look at the leaflets and fill in the information.**

stansted express

Stansted Express is a fast way to and from Stansted Airport, with trains every 15 or 30 minutes from Liverpool Street Station. And with a journey time of 45 minutes, the Stansted Express is a quick way to your destination. A single ticket costs £13.00.

For more information please click on 'service news' or call 0845 8500 150

Heathrow express

- **Heathrow Express** is a fast and convenient* way to travel between Heathrow Airport and London Paddington. It is a non-stop service and it takes only 15 minutes.
- With trains every 15 minutes, the **Heathrow Express** is better than any other form of transport.

Why not book online NOW?
Single tickets cost only £13.00.

For information call:
(+44) 845 600 1515

Luton Airport

With a modern airport and rail station, London Luton Airport is perfect for business and holiday travellers.

Thameslink takes you between London Bridge station and Luton Airport Parkway in 30 minutes. From the train station you catch the FREE bus, which takes you to the airport in five minutes.

- **Up to eight Thameslink trains an hour between London Bridge and Luton Airport Parkway**
- **Fast trains take 30 minutes to London**
- **£10.00 one way between London and Luton Airport Parkway**

gatwick express

The Gatwick Express is a high-speed train between Central London and Gatwick Airport. With a journey time of just 30 minutes from London Victoria Station to Gatwick (35 minutes on Sundays), there is no faster way between the city and the airport.

Why not book online now?
Single tickets cost £11.00.

Name of airport	Where do you arrive?	How long does it take?	How much does it cost?
Heathrow			
Gatwick			
Stansted			
Luton			

VOCABULARY CHECK LIST
What is it in your language? Find out!

busiest (*from* busy) ______

destinations ______

cheap ______

to get off ______

signs (a sign) ______

convenient ______

www.baa.co.uk/main/airports/heathrow

London Transport

Seven million people live in London. How do they travel?

London taxis

- London taxis are black.
- There are 18,300 black taxis in London.
- Taxi drivers take a test* called 'the knowledge' before they are taxi drivers. They study for two years to take this test.
- You can stop a taxi when the orange light* is on.
- All cars (but *not* black taxis) in London pay £5.00 a day (called 'the congestion charge') to drive into the centre.

London buses

- London buses are red.
- There are 20,000 buses in London.
- Oxford Street has more bus stops than any other street.
- Every day 4.5 million people go on a bus in London.
- In the centre of London you must buy your ticket before you get on* the bus.

Help the tourist!

There are many buses in London. Match the bus and its destination.

1. For the London Eye, take bus number one.
2. For Piccadilly Circus, take bus number eighty-eight.
3. For Tower Bridge, take bus forty-two.
4. For Big Ben, take bus one hundred and fifty-nine.
5. For Buckingham Palace, go to Victoria station. Take bus number eleven.

1 – e

....

....

....

....

a Buckingham Palace

b Big Ben

c Piccadilly Circus

d Tower Bridge

e The London Eye

The London Underground

- The underground is called 'the tube'.
- There are 275 stations in London.
- Every hour, 150,000 people go on the tube.
- Every year people leave 11,500 umbrellas on tube trains.
- Rats and mice live in the underground.

Tickets and Travelcards

Most Londoners don't buy single or return tickets. They have got travelcards. With a travelcard you can travel on buses, trains and the underground. You can buy a one-day, weekly, monthly or yearly travelcard. To buy a weekly, monthly or yearly travelcard, you need a photo.

Put the correct information in the weekly travel card.

Zones 1 2 3 • £27.00 • BMM 8141 • John Collins • ~~Mr~~ • (Photo) • weekly • 14 Aug 03

PHOTOCARD

Name: Miss / (Mr) / Mrs

....

....

....

BMM 8141

Travelcard

Number

Ticket type

Price

Date

Zones

Buying a ticket or travelcard. Read the dialogue.

The words *please* and *thank you* are not in the dialogue. Put them in the correct places.

Tourist: A one-day travelcard to London, ...

Travel assistant: That's £4.90 ....

Tourist: Here's £5.00.

Travel assistant: .... Here's your ticket and change.

Tourist: ....

VOCABULARY CHECK LIST
What is it in your language? Find out!

to take a test

light

to get on (the bus)

Act out the dialogue with your partner.

www.tfl.gov.uk/tfl/promotionintro.shtm

Going by Tube

Read the instructions and colour the Tube map. Start at the spot (•). Choose alternate* letters in the circles to find the name of each line*.

1 RED

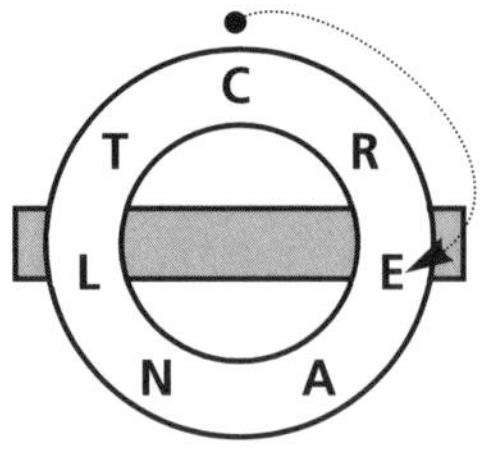

This line* runs through the centre of London and it joins Holland Park to Liverpool Street. Liverpool Street is also a railway station. This line goes under Oxford Street and the stations on Oxford Street are Marble Arch, Bond Street, Oxford Circus and Tottenham Court Road.

It's the ......Central...... Line.

2 YELLOW

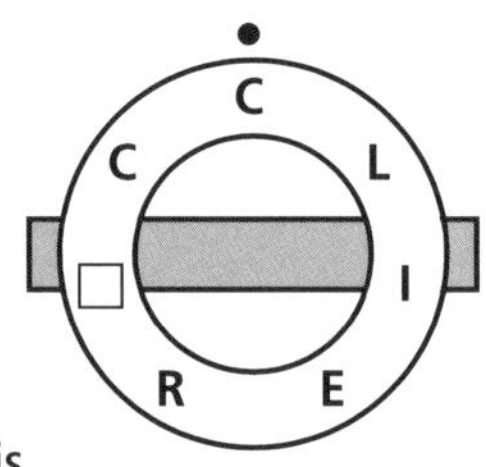

This line goes through Notting Hill Gate, Edgware Road, Barbican, Tower Hill, Embankment, Victoria, South Kensington, and back to Notting Hill Gate again. Tower Hill is the Tube stop* for the Tower of London. South Kensington is the Tube stop for the Science Museum and the Natural History Museum. Westminster is the Tube stop for the Houses of Parliament and Big Ben, and Notting Hill is the stop for Portobello Market.

It's the .... Line.

3 DARK BLUE

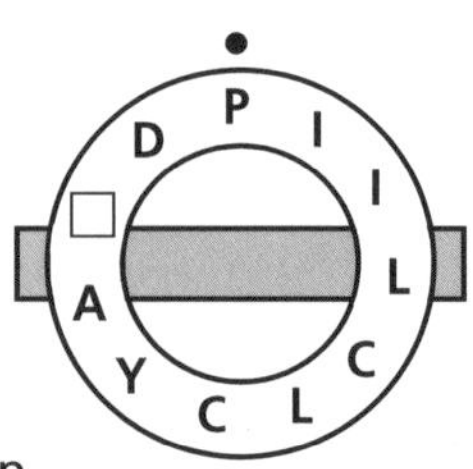

This line goes from King's Cross (a railway station) through Covent Garden, Piccadilly Circus, Leicester Square, Knightsbridge and Earl's Court. Knightsbridge is the Tube stop for Harrods. Piccadilly Circus and Leicester Square are in the West End. This is the name for the area* with theatres, cinemas, restaurants and shops. Heathrow Airport is at the end of this Tube line.

It's the .... Line.

4 LIGHT BLUE

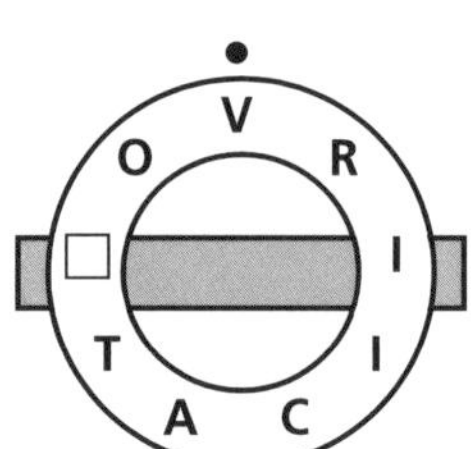

This line also goes through King's Cross. It goes through Oxford Street, Green Park and Victoria, and down to Pimlico. Pimlico is the Tube stop for Tate Britain. You can go from Tate Britain to Tate Modern (near St Paul's Cathedral) by boat. It's called *Tate to Tate*.

It's the .... Line.

5 BLACK

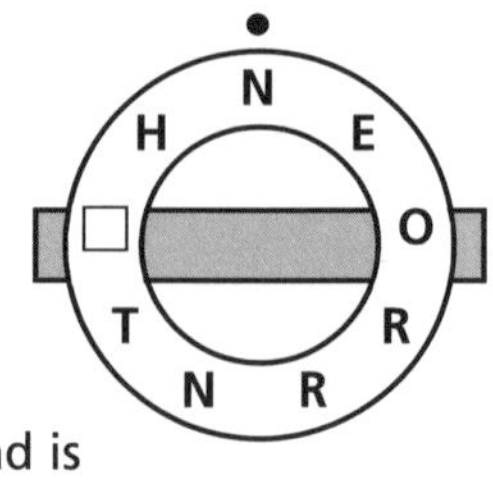

This line goes from Euston (a railway station) to Tottenham Court Road, Charing Cross (another railway station) and then to Waterloo. Tottenham Court Road is the stop for the British Museum. You can go by Eurostar train in Waterloo Station to France and Belgium. Another part* of this line goes from King's Cross, through Bank and on to London Bridge.

It's the .... Line.

6 GREEN

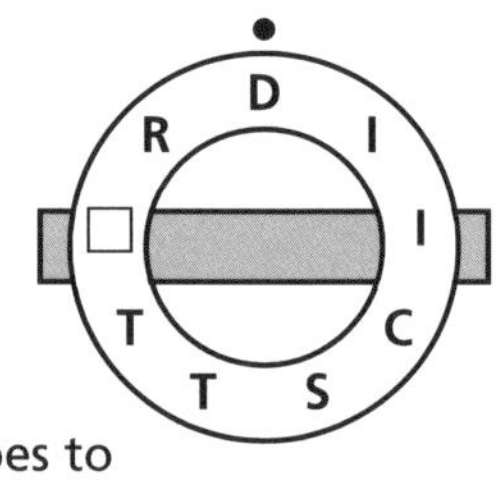

This line goes from Tower Hill through St James's Park to Earl's Court. After Earl's Court, one part goes to Wimbledon in the south (not on the map), and one part goes to Richmond (not on the map). From Earl's Court it goes up to Paddington (a railway station) and ends at Edgware Road. St James's Park is the Tube stop for Buckingham Palace.

It's the .... Line.

7 BROWN

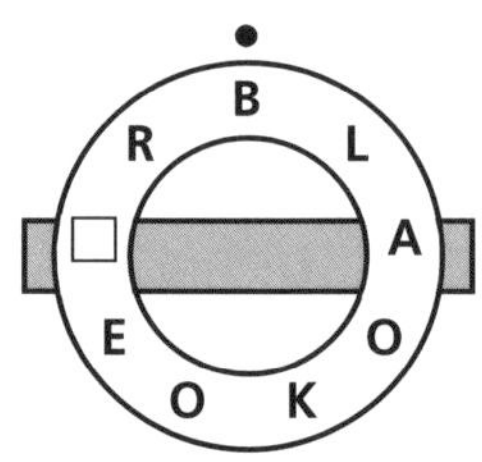

This line goes from Paddington, through Baker Street and Regent's Park and on to Waterloo. Baker Street is the Tube stop for Madame Tussauds Museum and Regent's Park is the Tube Station for London Zoo. Its name comes from two of the stations on the line.

It's the .... Line.

8 PINK

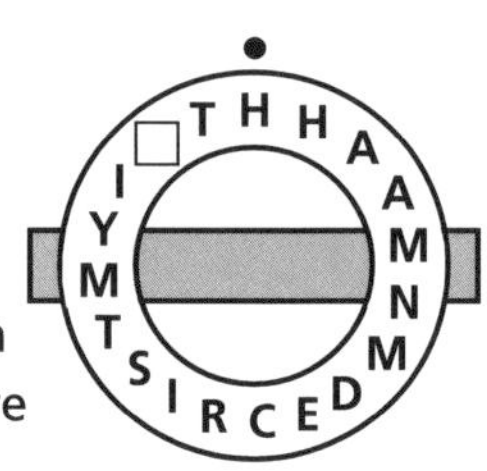

This line goes from Paddington to Baker Street, Barbican and Liverpool Street. The Barbican is an area of London with a large theatre and concert hall. The Museum of London is in the Barbican.

It's the .... Line.

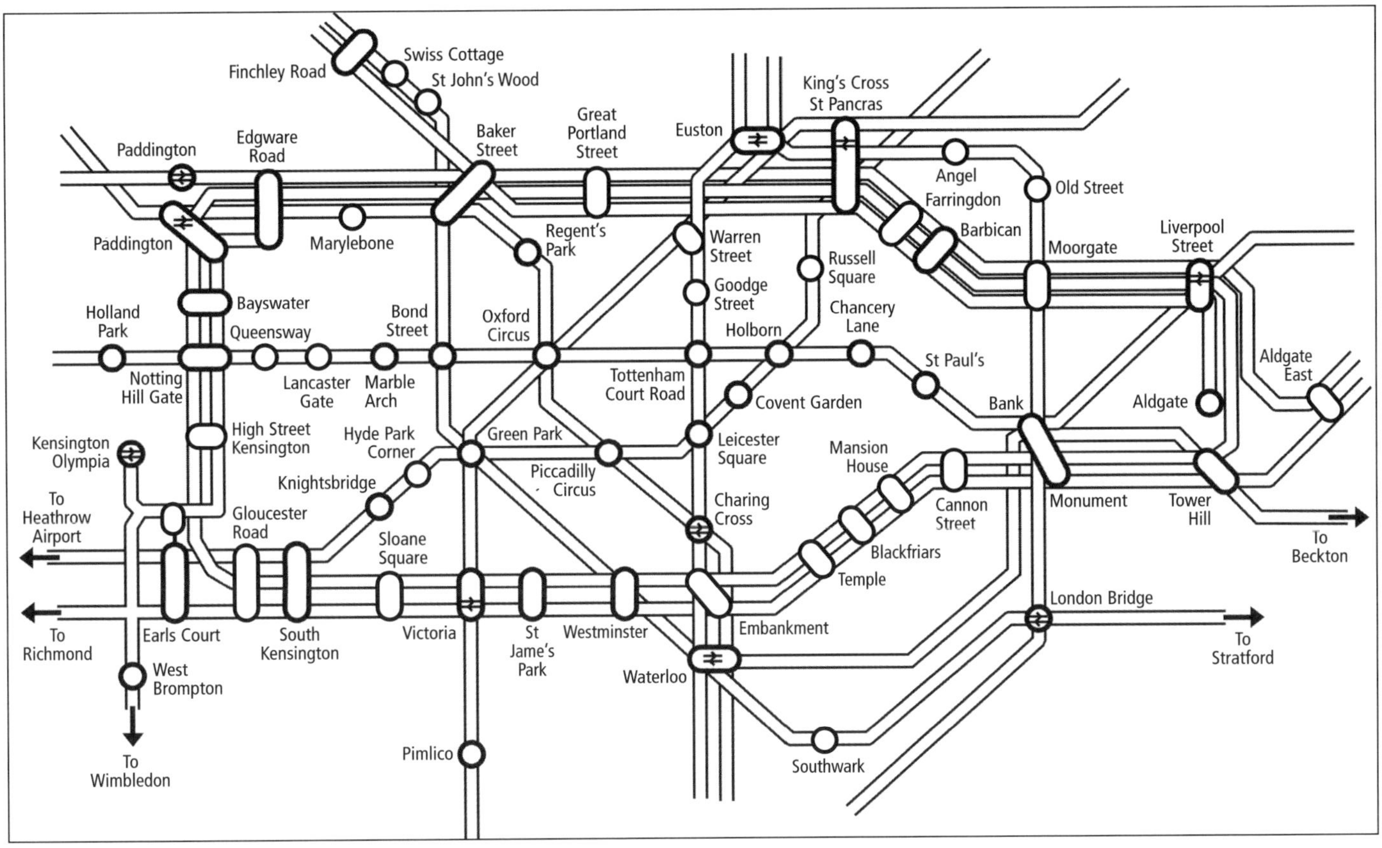

9 GREY

This line goes from Baker Street to Bond Street, Westminster, and on to Waterloo and London Bridge. It continues* east to Docklands, the area along the River Thames (not on the map).

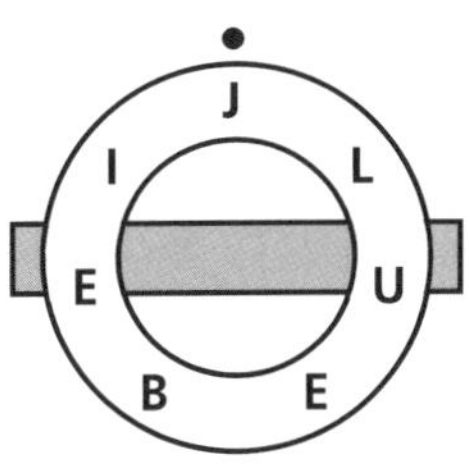

It's the .... Line.

10 PURPLE

This line goes from Aldgate and through Liverpool Street to Baker Street. After Baker Street it goes north to the suburbs* in the north west. You use this line to go to Wembley Arena for pop concerts.

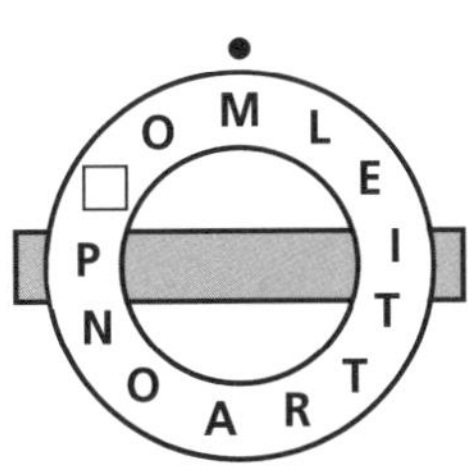

It's the .... Line.

11 ORANGE

This line has got two stops: Waterloo and Bank. It takes people to work in the City of London.

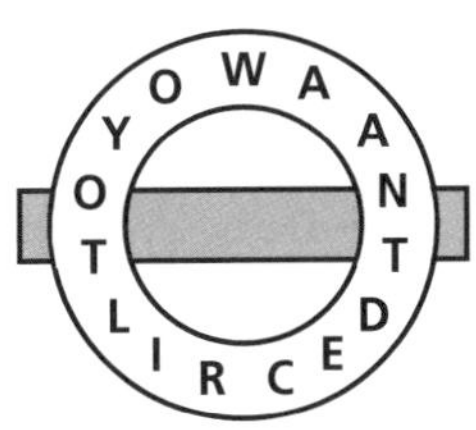

It's the .... Line.

12 WHITE

This line goes from Bank and also from Tower Hill and it goes to Docklands in the east of London.

It's the .... Line.

Finish these sentences:

a) St Paul's is .... stops from Tottenham Court Road.

b) Bayswater is between .... and ....

c) Hyde Park Corner is on the .... Line.

VOCABULARY CHECK LIST

What is it in your language? Find out!

alternate	part
line	to continue
stop	suburb
area	

www.londontransport.co.uk

The London Eye

If you want to see London, the best place to go is the Eye. The Eye is a big wheel* on the River Thames.

The Eye is very popular. Every day 1600 people go on the Eye. There are 33 capsules* and one ride takes 30 minutes.

The Eye is very tall – 133 metres. At the top of the Eye you get a great view* of London. You can see for 25 miles (40 kilometres) but don't go if you are afraid of* heights*!

A great view!

At the top of the Eye you can see many places in London. Here are 5 things you can see from the Eye. Match the word halves to make these London icons.

1

2

1 Trafalgar — Square
2 Tower
3 Big
4 St. Paul's
5 A black

Ben
Square
Cathedral
taxi
Bridge

5

4

3

Imagine you are 133 metres high in your town / city. What places can you see?

....

....

How much does it cost?

You want to visit the London Eye. Here is the London Eye price list.

The London Eye Price list

Adult:	£11.00
Child (5-15 years):	£5.50
Under fives:	free
Senior (over 60 years):	£10.00
Group ticket (10 people):	£100.00
Romantic flight with champagne:	£40.00

We accept credit cards

Look at these five different groups of people.
How much does it cost them to go on the Eye?

1 £ ....

2 £ ....

3 £ ....

4 £ ....

5 £ ....

These were the prices at the time of publishing this book. Go to the Internet site **www.londoneye.com** and click on "plan your visit" and then "prices". Find out how much the prices are.

You don't need to book tickets. You can buy tickets on the day for the Eye. Work in pairs. One of you works at the Eye and one of you is a visitor. Imagine you are taking your family / friends on the Eye. Ask for tickets. How much do they cost?

VOCABULARY CHECK LIST
What is it in your language? Find out!

wheel ____________

capsule ____________

view ____________

to be afraid of ____________

heights ____________

www.londoneye.com

The Tower of London

The Tower of London is London's oldest castle*. It's nine hundred years old. It's got Beefeaters, ravens, the crown jewels and ghosts...!

Beefeaters

Beefeaters don't eat beef! They protect* the Tower. The name 'Beefeater' comes from when the Queen gave them meat, not money, as their pay. Beefeaters like the name Yeoman Warders. Forty Beefeaters (or Yeoman Warders) live at the Tower.

I want to live at the Tower. ☐

I don't want to live at the Tower. ☐

Ravens*

They are scary birds. There are seven ravens here. If they leave the Tower it is very bad luck. Every day the ravens eat meat, eggs and biscuits with blood*. Yuk!

I like the ravens. ☐

I don't like the ravens. ☐

The Crown Jewels

The Crown Jewels are in the Jewel Room. The royal crown has got three hundred jewels on it, but the Queen only wears the crown once* every year!

What jewellery have you got?

I've got ____________________

Ghosts

The Tower has got many ghosts. There are ghosts in the Salt Tower. Dogs don't like to go in the Salt Tower and Beefeaters don't like to go in there at night.

Are you afraid of ghosts?

Yes ☐ **No** ☐

Numbers search

Find these numbers in the text.

A 300 | B 7 | C 900 | D 40

Escape from the Tower

You are a prisoner*. You want to escape from the Tower.
Read the sentences and go to the correct key in the Tower. Draw your route on the map.

1. Take key number ten.
2. Go to key number fifteen. Run! There are Beefeaters here!
3. Go in the room. You see the crown. Take key eighty-eight and the crown.
4. Go to key thirty. Open the door.
5. Oh no! Ghosts! Run to key seventy-two.
6. You see a Beefeater. He is sleeping. Take key ninety-nine. Open the door and run!

VOCABULARY CHECK LIST
What is it in your language? Find out!

castle	blood
to protect	once
ravens	prisoner

www.hrp.org.uk/webcode/tower_home.asp

The River Thames

London is the home of England's most famous and important river: the Thames. Many important places in London are next to the Thames. You can find the Houses of Parliament, the Tower of London and the London Eye on the riverside.

- The Thames is a short river. It's only 349 km long. The Amazon, in Brazil is 6,437 km long!
- Many people think the Thames is not clean but this is not true. More than 97 types of fish live here, for example salmon* and eels*. Eels are a traditional food in East London. People make a pie and serve it with mashed potatoes*. It's called 'eel pie and mash'.
- Two years ago, a dolphin* was in the Thames!

What's the name of the river in your capital city?

....

How long is it?

It's .... long.

Frogtours!

How do you go sightseeing without all the traffic? You can take a Frogtour. A frogboat is a tank for tourists. It travels on the road and on the river...but be careful – you get wet* on this tour!

You are on a frogboat in the Thames. Listen to your captain, draw the route and write the letters of the places you see in the correct boxes.

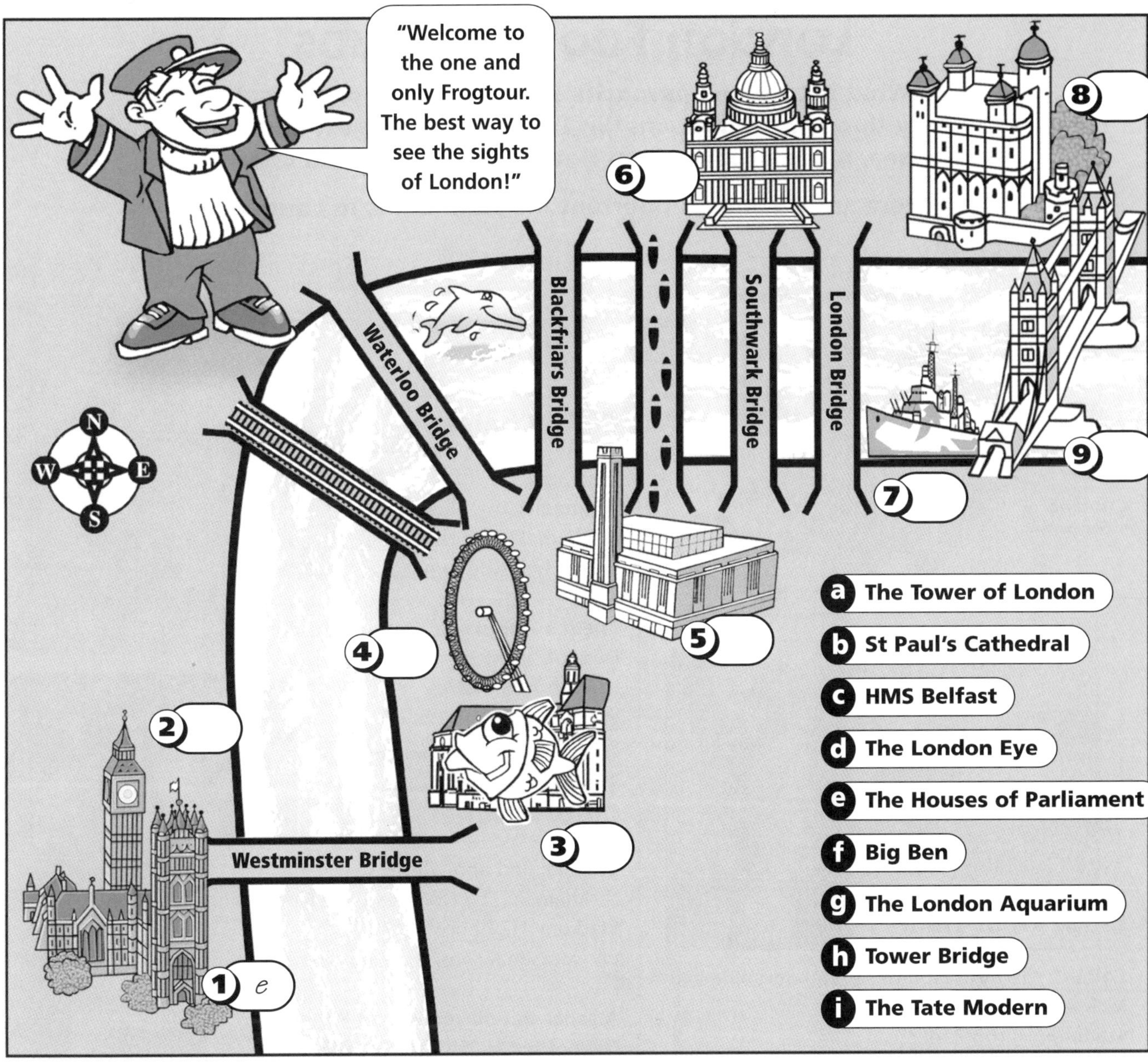

- Before we go *under* Westminster Bridge, you can see the Houses of Parliament. You can hear Big Ben!
- Do you like fish? *Opposite* The Houses of Parliament is the London Aquarium.
- *Next to* the Aquarium is The London Eye. You get the best view of London here!
- Now we're going *under* four bridges. One bridge is for walking only. On the south side there is Tate Modern, an art gallery. On the north side you can see St Paul's Cathedral.
- We're going *under* two bridges. You can see a large ship in front of us. This is HMS Belfast, it's a museum ship.
- *Opposite* HMS Belfast is the home of the Crown Jewels and the Beefeaters. This is the Tower of London. Now we're stopping here *in front of* London's most beautiful bridge, Tower Bridge.

VOCABULARY CHECK LIST **What is it in your language? Find out!**

salmon	eel	mashed potato	dolphin	to get wet

www.frogtours.com

London Football Clubs

What is London's favourite sport? Football of course!
There are twenty-three football teams* in London. The biggest and most popular are Chelsea, Arsenal, Tottenham Hotspur, West Ham and Charlton.

Here are the most important football teams in London.

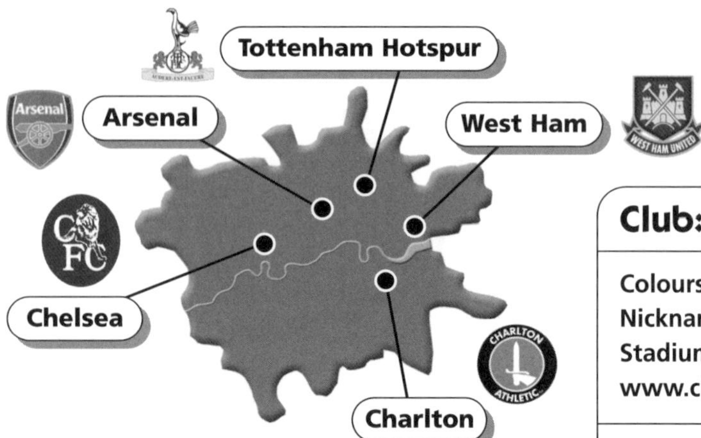

Club: Chelsea

Colours: Blue
Nickname: The Blues
Stadium: Stamford Bridge
www.chelseafc.com

Chelsea star player: Hernan Crespo
Date of birth: 5th July 1975
Height: 1.85 metres
Weight: 78 kilograms

Club: West Ham

Colours: Claret (a kind of purple) and blue
Nickname: The Hammers
Stadium: Upton Park
www.whufc.com

West Ham star ex-player: David James
Date of birth: 1st August 1970
Height: 1.96 metres
Weight: 91.25 kilograms

Club: Arsenal

Colours: Red and white
Nickname*: The Gunners / The Gooners
Stadium: Highbury
www.arsenal.com

Arsenal star player: Robert Pires
Date of birth: 29 October 1973
Height: 1.88 metres
Weight: 74 kilograms

Club: Tottenham Hotspur

Colours: White and blue
Nickname: Spurs
Stadium: White Hart Lane
www.spurs.co.uk

Spurs star player: Robbie Keane
Date of birth: 8th July 1980
Height: 1.75 metres
Weight: 63.56 kilograms

Which player ...

1 ...is the tallest?

....

2 ...is the oldest?

....

3 ...is the heaviest*?

....

4 ...has got the longest hair?

....

Mascots

Most football clubs have mascots*.
Here are four mascots from the London clubs.
Can you match them to their clubs?

a) West Ham
b) Arsenal
c) Tottenham Hotspur
d) Chelsea

1 Gunnersaurus Rex ◯

2 Stamford the Lion ◯

3 Chirpy Cockrell ◯

4 Herbie Hammer ◯

The Fans

Here are two West Ham fans
and two Arsenal fans.
What do you think they are saying?

____

____

Football chants*

Here are three chants. Which clubs do you hear them at?

1 Carefree
Wherever you may be
We are the famous CFC

____

2 Come on you Spurs!

____

3 Up the Irons!

____

VOCABULARY CHECK LIST What is it in your language? Find out!

team	nickname	heaviest	mascot	chant

Madame Tussauds

There are more than one hundred museums in London. The most popular museum is Madame Tussauds, the waxwork* museum. It has so many visitors that you can wait for up to an hour in the queue*.

At Madame Tussauds you can meet hundreds of famous people in one day. It's got wax models of pop stars, sports stars, film stars and politicians. It's even got a Chamber of Horrors, with famous criminals*... Don't go there if you are afraid*!

Look at these four wax models. Which famous people are they?

1 He's American.
He's a politician.
It's ....

2 She's Australian.
She's a pop singer.
It's ....

3 He's English.
He's a football player.
It's ....

4 She's a Latino.
She's a singer and an actress.
It's ....

Do you think the wax figures look like the real famous people?

1. It looks like him. ☐
   It doesn't look like him. ☐
2. It looks like her. ☐
   It doesn't look like her. ☐
3. It looks like him. ☐
   It doesn't look like him. ☐
4. It looks like her. ☐
   It doesn't look like her. ☐

Do you look like a famous person?

I look like ....

In the modelling room

You are in the wax work modelling room. You find lots of body parts. Which famous person's waxwork do they belong to?

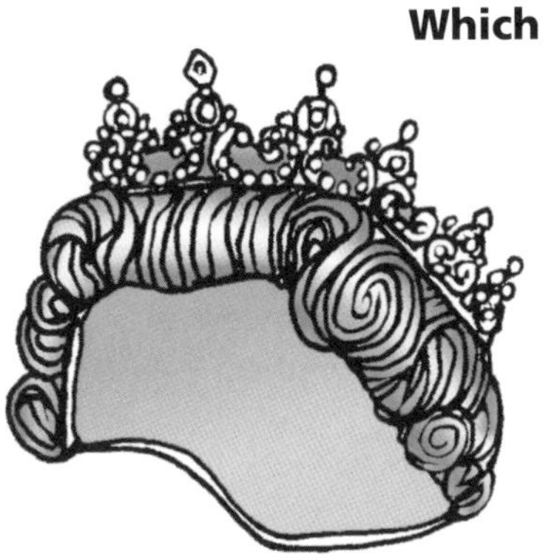

1. It's ...The Queen's... hair.
2. It's .... arm.

3. It's .... moustache.
4. They're .... legs.

Now work in pairs. Draw a famous person's body part. Your partner must guess who it is, e.g. *Is it Spiderman's arm? Is it J-Lo's hair?*

VOCABULARY CHECK LIST

What is it in your language? Find out!

waxwork
☐
queue
☐
criminals
☐
to be afraid
☐

www.madame-tussauds.com

Buckingham Palace

Would you like to live in a house with 600 rooms, 78 bathrooms, a cinema, a swimming pool and a post office?

This is the Queen's London home, Buckingham Palace. The Queen has four other palaces in Britain, but this is her most famous home. If the Queen's flag* is flying outside the palace, it means that the Queen is at home. If you are in London between August and October, you can go inside Buckingham Palace. You can see the State dining room, ballroom, the Queen's gallery with all her paintings* and the mews where the royal coaches* and horses are. But you can't see all of the rooms. The palace is too big!

Look at the picture of the Palace. Read the description to find out which room it is.

a) Gallery **b)** Ballroom **c)** Cinema **d)** Post office **e)** State dining room **f)** Swimming pool **g)** Balcony

1 In this room, the Queen and her family can watch TV and movies. c

2 This room is very big. This is where the Queen has all of her paintings. ☐

3 In this room there is a table where 60 people can sit and eat. ☐

Front view of Buckingham Palace

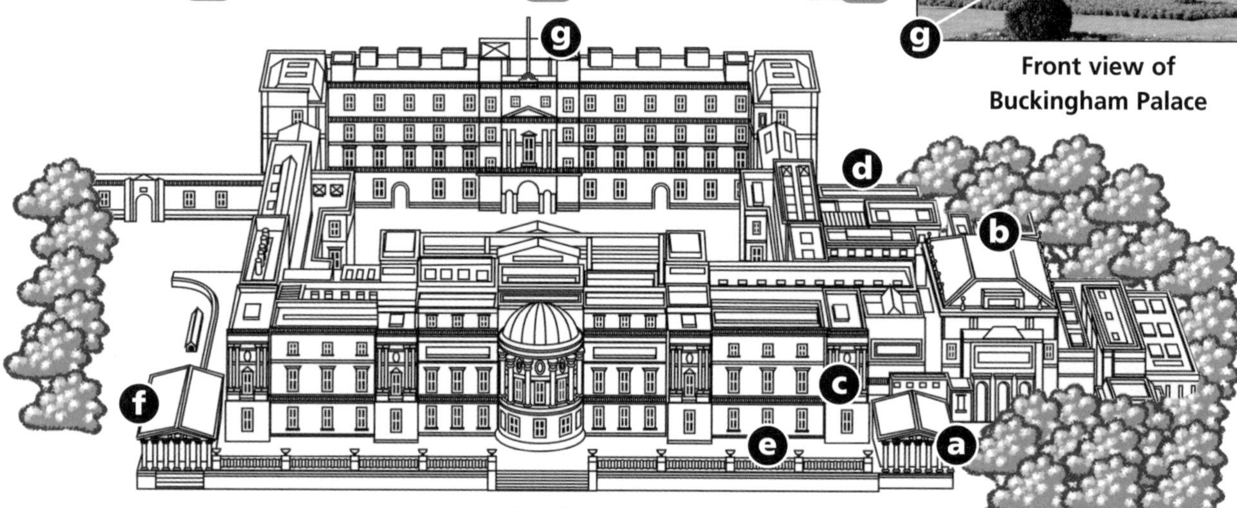

Back view of Buckingham Palace

4 This room is where the Queen and her visitors can dance. ☐

5 This is where the Queen gets letters and mail. ☐

6 This is where the Queen stands when she waves to the public. ☐

7 This is where the Queen goes swimming. ☐

Is your house better than the Queen's?

Buckingham Palace	My House
600 rooms	
78 bathrooms	
300 clocks	
A dining table for 60 people	
A swimming pool	
A cinema	
A 40-acre garden	
A lake	

VOCABULARY CHECK LIST

What is it in your language? Find out!

flag ☐

paintings ☐

coaches ☐

www.vrbritain.com

The London Butterfly House

The Butterfly House is in the garden of Syon House on the River Thames in west London. You can see tropical* butterflies from all over the world (Costa Rica, Argentina, Tanzania, Thailand, Indonesia, Australia and the Philippines).

The butterflies are in a big glass* house and they can fly everywhere*. Visitors can walk among them as they feed* and fly. Some of the butterflies like to sit on your head or shoulders! You can see the big cages* where the caterpillars live. Caterpillars have strong mouths, six legs, but no eyes. Caterpillars love eating and eat a lot of leaves. You can see other cages with chrysalises* in them where the caterpillars 'sleep' and become butterflies. When a new butterfly comes out of the chrysalis after two or three weeks, its wings are wet and it can't fly because it must wait until blood* gets into the wings. Female butterflies are bigger than males. It's hot and damp* in the Butterfly House because the temperature is always 28° and the butterflies can't live in dry air or in winds. They need damp air. There are lizards, iguanas, scorpions and spiders there, too. You can also the world's biggest snail* – it's 25cm long!

Find the Butterflies

Follow the colour key and colour the butterflies. Then, read the descriptions of each of the butterflies and write the names under the pictures.

1 = brown **2** = blue **3** = white **4** = red **5** = yellow **6** = grey
7 = black **8** = green **9** = orange **10** = pink

1

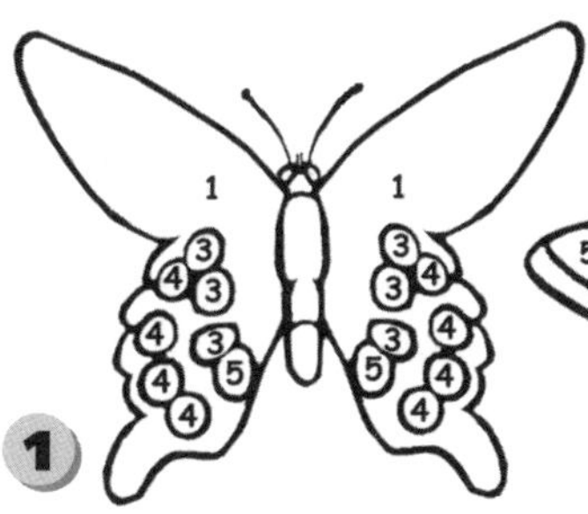

....

2

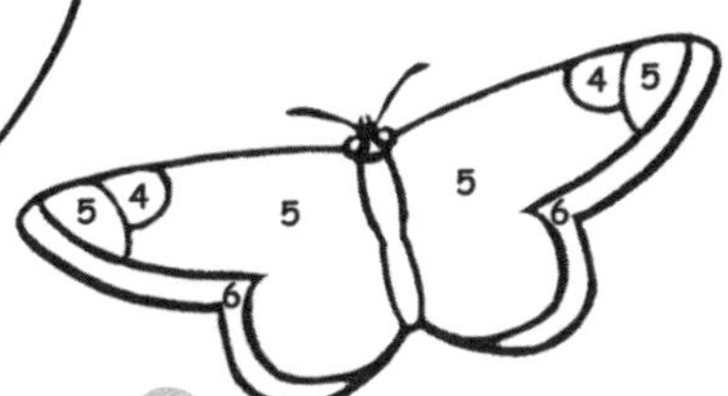

....

3

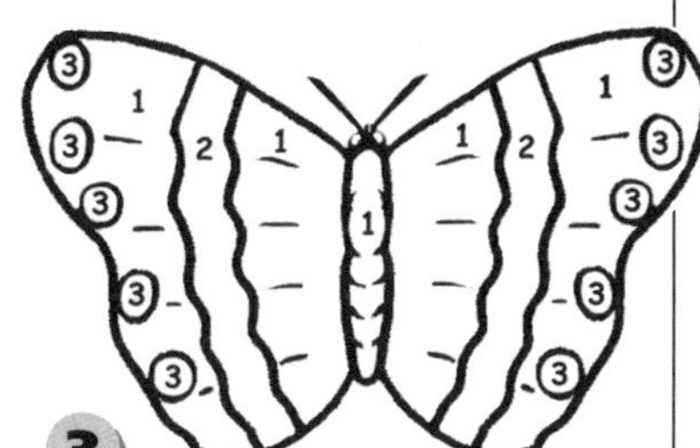

....

4

....

5

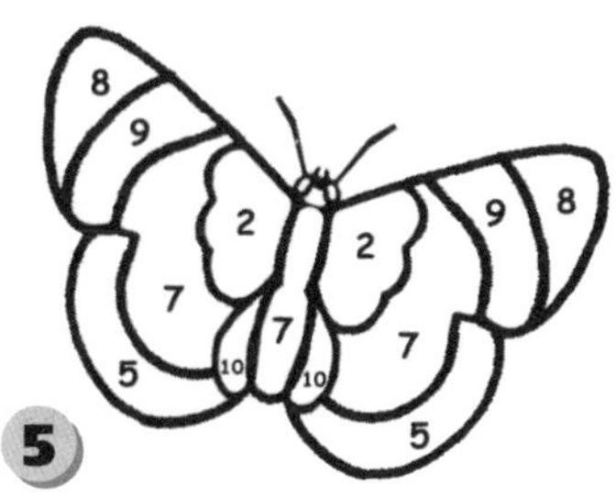

....

6

....

a) The BANDED SOLDIER is red with black stripes*.
b) The ROSE BUTTERFLY is brown with four red spots*, three white spots and a yellow spot on its two back wings.
c) The ACHILLES BUTTERFLY is brown with a large blue stripe and small white spots on its wings.
d) The SAPPHIRE BUTTERFLY has got green, orange, black and yellow strips on its wings. Near the body, the wings are blue and there are small pink stripes on the back wings.
e) The RODRIGUEZ AGRIAS BUTTERFLY has got grey and blue back wings and grey, blue and red front wings.
f) The MONARCH BUTTERFLY is yellow with red, grey and yellow spots on the ends of the wings.

VOCABULARY CHECK LIST

What is it in your language? Find out!

- tropical ____
- glass ____
- everywhere ____
- to feed ____
- cage ____
- chrysalis ____
- blood ____
- damp ____
- snail ____
- stripe ____
- spot ____

www.butterflies.org.uk/

Hamleys

Hamleys is the most famous toy shop in the world. It's in Regent Street.

- Hamleys is old! It's 243 years old.
- Hamleys is popular all year but at Christmas it's very busy – two million people come here in the weeks before Christmas.
- Many famous people come to Hamleys. David and Victoria Beckham are fans.
- 4,500 people work at Hamleys.

Which floor?

Hamleys has got seven floors* of toys. Look at the floor guide*.

Hamleys

Basement*

Computer world; computer games; PlayStation; street sports; bikes.

Ground floor*

Soft toys; teddy bears; magic; toilets

First Floor

Sweet factory; games; jigsaws; science

Second Floor

Books; music; bathtime; pre-school

Third Floor

Dolls; prams; dolls' houses; art

Fourth Floor

Trains; Corgi cars; remote control cars*; soldiers

Fifth Floor

Star Wars; Spiderman; Lego; café; toilets

Which floor(s) do you go to if you would like....

1 to eat something? ....

2 to buy a skateboard? ....

3 to buy some sweets? ....

4 to buy something for a girl? ....

5 to buy something for a two-year-old? ....

Which floor would *you* like to go to?

I'd like to go to the ....

Speaking

In the shop: work in pairs

One of you is the shop assistant, one of you is the customer.

Customer: Look at the pictures 1-6. Ask where these toys are.
e.g. *Excuse me, where are the computer games?*

Assistant: Look at your floor guide and reply
e.g. *They are on the first / second / third,* etc, *floor.*

1

2

3

4

5

6

Every year there is a new toy craze*.
Design a toy that every child will want and describe it.

....

....

....

VOCABULARY CHECK LIST
What is it in your language? Find out!

floor ______

guide ______

basement ______

ground floor ______

remote control car ______

craze ______

www.hamleys.co.uk

Harrods

Welcome to the biggest department store* in Europe – Harrods.

- If you want to go shopping in London, one of the best places is Harrods.
- Harrods sells everything. There are 330 departments and you can buy anything here: a plane, a four-poster bed* for your dog, or an elephant!
- Harrods is one of the busiest shops in London. Every day 35,000 people visit Harrods and more than 4,000 people work there.

Rules of the store

Harrods has strict rules*. You can see lots of signs on the doors. The signs tell customers what they *can* / *can't* do in the shop.

Look at these 6 signs and circle the correct word.

You **can** / **can't** take photos in the shop.

1

You **can** / **can't** eat ice-cream or hamburgers in the shop.

2

Many people in Harrods **can** / **can't** speak two languages. You can speak French, Spanish, German, etc to them.

3

You **can** / **can't** carry a rucksack* in the shop.

4

You **can** / **can't** pay with credit cards*.

5

You **can** / **can't** wear swimwear or shorts in the shop.

6

Problems, problems!

If you buy something in Harrods and there is a problem with it, you can take it back. Harrods can give you the money (a refund*) or something of the same price (an exchange*). But you must have the receipt.

Here are five things. What's the matter with these things?

1 It's ...*too big*......

2 They are ....

3 My mother ....

4 It's got ....

5 It's ....

Take it back!

Put these phrases in the correct speech bubbles.

It's too big.
OK. What's the problem with it?
That's fine. Have you got the receipt?
Yes, it's this jumper.
Yes, here it is.
I'd like an exchange. I'd like this jumper in a smaller size.

Can I help you? → [ ]

[ ] → [ ]

Would you like an exchange or refund? → [ ]

[ ] → [ ]

Now practise the role-play with a partner. Use the problems.

VOCABULARY CHECK LIST

What is it in your language? Find out!

department store	rucksack	refund
four-poster bed	credit card	exchange
rules		

www.harrods.com

London Markets

London has got more than 65 street markets where you can buy everything and anything. The two most popular markets in London are Covent Garden market and Camden market.

Covent Garden

Covent Garden was* the biggest fruit and vegetable market in England but now it's got more than bananas. Now it's got hundreds of shops, stalls*, restaurants and bars. You can buy almost anything here!

Street Theatre

If you don't like shopping, you can watch the coolest* street artists in Covent Garden. The best street artists in the world come here. You can see jugglers*, dancers, mime* artists and people on stilts* and unicycles*. Watch out for the fire-eaters!

Can you...?	I can	I can't
juggle with two oranges?	☐	☐
juggle with three oranges?	☐	☐
stand still without moving?	☐	☐
ride a unicycle?	☐	☐
play two musical instruments at the same time?	☐	☐

Camden Market

Camden market is the fourth most popular tourist attraction in London. Camden is like four different markets in one place. Camden is famous for its cool street fashions, vegetarian food, music stalls and jewellery. There are more tattoo* and piercing* shops here than in any other part of London. And if you don't want to shop, buy music or get a tattoo, it's a great place for people-watching!

Here are five other famous London markets. Match the markets to their photos on the next page.

1 Billingsgate market

(5.00 am – 8.00 am)
Do you like fish? Billingsgate is not a market for tourists. This market sells fish. It's the smelliest* market in London!

2 Columbia Road market

Roses, carnations, daises... they are all here. This is the best market to go to if you love flowers. It smells beautiful!

3 Portobello Road

(7.00 am – 6.00 pm)
Do you like collecting* things? You can buy old stamps, coins, medals and antiques here.

4 Brixton market

Brixton market is in south London. You can buy lots of Jamaican food but you can buy clothes here too.

5 Petticoat Lane market

(Sundays)
This is the oldest market in London. It's over 400 years old. It is famous for its clothes and lace* and is in East London.

a

b

c

d

e

Which market would you like to go to?

I'd like to go to

....

At the market

You are at Camden Market in London.
Look at the questions and tick (✓) the correct word (*is* or *are*).
The correct answers move you to the correct stall.

1 How much ___ the CD?
are ☐ move 1 ←
is ☐ move 1 →
£ 10.00

2 How much ___ the jacket?
are ☐ move 1 →
is ☐ move 2 ←
£ ....

3 How much ___ the hot dogs?
are ☐ move 4 →
is ☐ move 3 ←
£ ....

4 How much ___ the strawberries?
is ☐ move 2 →
are ☐ move 1 ←
£ ....

5 How much ___ the old clock?
is ☐ move 4 ←
are ☐ move 1 →
£ ....

6 How much ___ the boots?
is ☐ move 4 →
are ☐ move 1 ←
£ ....

Now write the correct prices in the boxes.

£20.00	**£60.00**	**£25.00**	**Start here**	**£10.00**	**£0.30**	**£1.50**

VOCABULARY CHECK LIST

What is it in your language? Find out!

- was
- stall
- cool (coolest)
- juggler (to juggle)
- to mime
- stilts
- unicycle
- tattoo
- piercing
- smelliest (smelly)
- to collect
- lace

www.eastlondonmarkets.com

London's Theatreland

If you come to London you must spend one night at the theatre!

In London there are 51 theatres and every year 11 million people come to watch a play or a show. You can see everything here – opera, comedy, drama, dance and musicals.

What's your favourite thing to see at the theatre?

Opera ☐ A comedy show ☐ Drama ☐ Dance ☐ A musical ☐

Most of the theatres are in Piccadilly or the Covent Garden area. The oldest and most famous theatre is the Theatre Royal.

If you buy a ticket you might get more than you think! People think that there is a ghost* in the theatre. 200 years ago people found a secret room. In the room there was a skeleton* with a dagger* in it. Many people say they see a ghost, but they only see it if they go to a daytime show (a matinée).

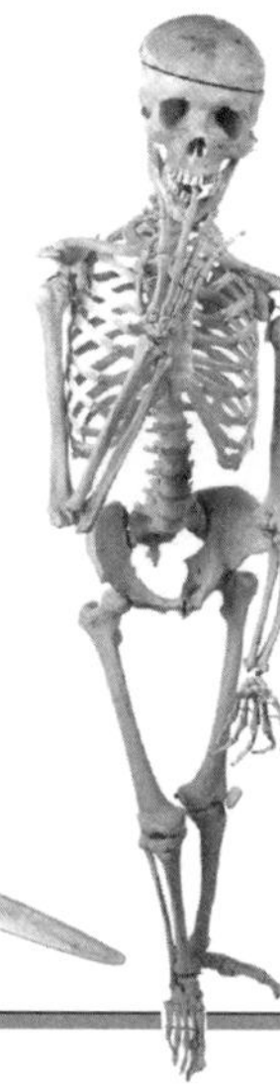

London musicals

The most popular shows in London are musicals. Here are London's top musicals. Look at the titles of the musicals and match them to their stories.

1 ____

2 ____

3 ____

4 ____

5 ____

6 ____

7 ____

a) This is the story of an ugly old composer* who lives under an opera house in Paris. He is in love with a beautiful opera singer.

b) This is the story of a group of students who want to sing, dance and be famous. They go to the New York School of Performing Arts.

c) This is the story of an inventor and his family. They have many adventures in their car that can fly.

d) This story is in Africa. It's about Simba the lion.

e) This story is about a simple London girl who sells flowers. She meets Henry Higgins who wants to teach her how to become a 'lady'.

f) This was a film. It's about two teenagers, Sandy and Danny who fall in love* on holiday. When they meet again at school, love is not so easy!

g) This musical was a film with Catherine Zeta-Jones and Renée Zellweger. It's the story of two dancers, Roxie and Velma in America in the 1920s.

Which musical would you like to see? I'd like to see ....

At the box office

Musicals are very popular. It's not easy to get a ticket. For the most popular shows you can wait for six months to a year to see a show!

There are three different types of ticket:

Stalls

These are the expensive seats. They are on the ground floor in front of the stage.

Circle

These are above the stalls. The front rows are expensive but the other rows are cheaper than the stalls.

Balcony

These seats are the cheapest seats. They have a very good view but the seats are high. If you are afraid of heights, or have bad eyesight don't go!

They will also ask you:
"Matinée or evening?"

Booking a ticket

Here are some things you say and hear when you are booking tickets for a show. Choose the option that is grammatically correct.

1
a) Hello. Theatre Royal box office, can I help you? ☐
b) Hello. Theatre Royal box office, can't I help you? ☐

2
a) Hello. I can to book ticket for The Lion King, please? ☐
b) Hello. Can I book tickets for The Lion King, please? ☐

3
a) I'd like tickets for January. ☐
b) I like tickets for the January. ☐

4
a) Are you like stalls, circle or balcony? ☐
b) Would you like stalls, circle, or balcony? ☐

5
a) We like two tickets in the stalls, please. ☐
b) We'd like two tickets in the stalls, please. ☐

6
a) What time does the show start? ☐
b) What time starts the show? ☐

7
a) Can I pay by credit card? ☐
b) Can I paying by credit card? ☐

Speaking

Now make your own dialogue to book a ticket for a musical. Use the sentences above to help you.

VOCABULARY CHECK LIST What is it in your language? Find out!

ghost	skeleton	dagger	composer	to fall in love

www.officiallondontheatre.co.uk/shows

Dogs in London

Battersea Dogs' Home is a famous home for lost* or abandoned* dogs and cats in London. It's nearly 150 years old.

Battersea Dogs Home

Every day 27 dogs come to the Home. That's about 10,000 every year! The Home gives dogs and cats a place to sleep, medicine, food and love. It tries to find good homes for the dogs.

Spot the dog

Here are three of the dogs in the Home at the moment. Match the description to the dog.

a

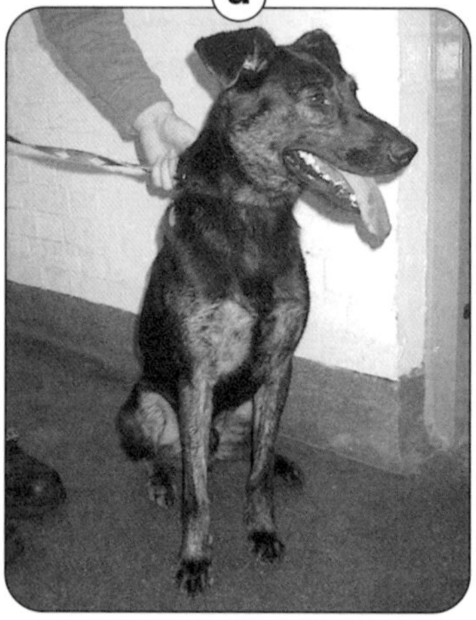

b

c

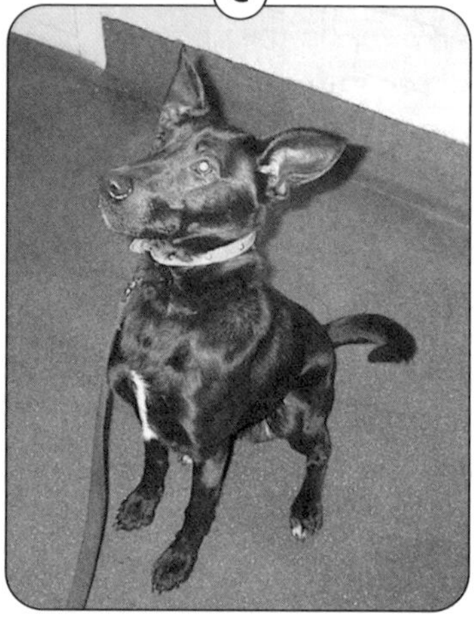

1. I'm Rosie Baby. I'm two years old. I'm small and white with brown ears. I like toys, games and walks. ☐

2. I'm Bob. I'm eighteen months old. I'm small and black with a white stomach. I like biscuits and treats*. I don't like cats. ☐

3. I'm Nova. I'm very intelligent. I'm big. I'm brown and black. I like walks. ☐

Pet Quiz! Do you know?

1	What's the most popular pet in Britain?	☐ **a)** rabbit	☐ **b)** dog	☐ **c)** cat
2	What's the most popular pet in the world?	☐ **a)** canary	☐ **b)** dog	☐ **c)** hamster
3	How many people own dogs in Britain?	☐ **a)** 10 million	☐ **b)** 6 million	☐ **c)** 8 million
4	Which pet lives the longest?	☐ **a)** goldfish	☐ **b)** dog	☐ **c)** canary
5	What's the most popular breed of dog in Britain?	☐ **a)** poodle	☐ **b)** Alsatian	☐ **c)** Labrador
6	In which country was the first dog show held in 1859?	☐ **a)** France	☐ **b)** Britain	☐ **c)** America

Where's Sam?

Your dog is missing*. You telephone Battersea Dogs' Home.

Assistant: Hello. Battersea Dogs' Home.

You: Oh hello. Our dog's missing. We want to check if it's in the Home.

Assistant: Oh dear. When did you lose your dog?

You: Two days ago. On Wednesday.

Assistant: Has it got microchip identity? Or a collar*?

You: No. He's called Sam.

Assistant: OK. Describe him to me.

You: He's four years old. He's small and black with a white ear and a white tail.

Assistant: OK. We'll have a look. Which ear is white?

You: The left ear.

Assistant: OK. Can you call me back in an hour?

You: Of course. Thank you.

Look at these dogs. Can you find Sam?

Work in pairs. One of you works at the Dogs' Home; one of you can't find your dog. Telephone Battersea Dogs' Home.

Did you know...?

The first dog to go to space was Laika in 1957. She was from Russia and died on the trip.

The oldest cat in the world lives in the UK. She is 31 and her name is Fluff.

The most expensive cat in the world cost £25,000 (€15, 625). His name was Cato and he was a Bengal cat.

VOCABULARY CHECK LIST What is it in your language? Find out!

lost	abandoned	treats	to be missing	collar

www.dogshome.org

Eating Out: London Food

You are never far* from a restaurant in London.
London has got more than 10,000 restaurants, so you can't get hungry!

Here are some of the foods you can find in London.

Look at these seven dishes. What are they?

pizza • cheeseburger • fish and chips
sushi • curry • noodles

1 ....

2 ....

3 ....

4 ....

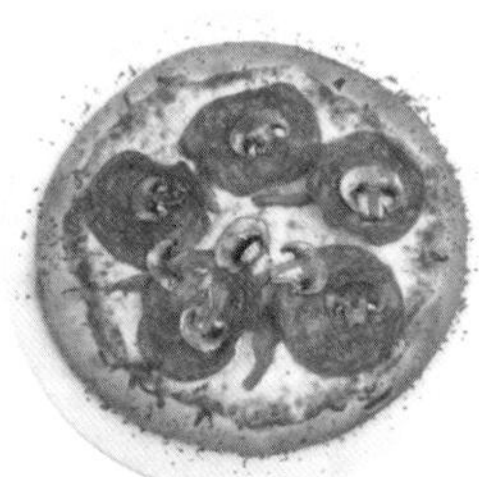

5 ....

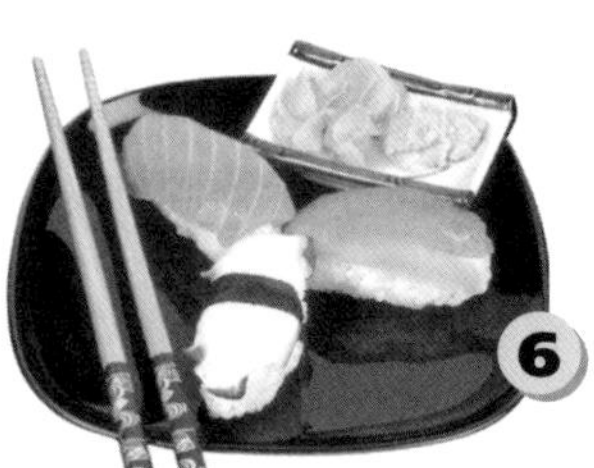

6 ....

Which one is your favourite?

....

Pie* and Mash

What is London's traditional dish? It's pie and mash (mashed potatoes). This is a traditional East End dish. What's in the pie? Eels*! There are lots of eels in the River Thames. Not many Londoners eat eel pie and mash though!

Fish and Chips

Not everybody likes pie and mash but everybody loves fish and chips! The oldest fish and chip shop in London is the *Rock and Sole Plaice*. It's more than 130 years old. Most English people love to eat fish and chips with salt and lots of vinegar*.

What do people eat with their chips in your country?

salt ☐ ketchup ☐ mayonnaise ☐ vinegar ☐

When you get your chips, the assistant sometimes says "Open or wrapped*?"

What do you think this means?

....

Chinatown

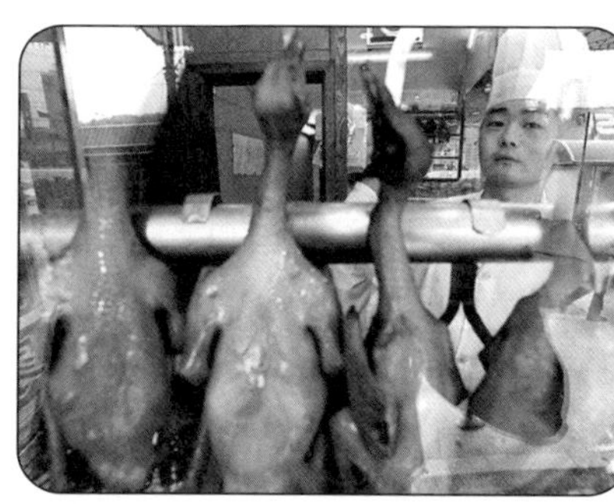

In England, Chinese food is the most popular takeaway*. The most popular dish is lemon chicken. In the centre of London there is an area called Chinatown. There are many Chinese restaurants and Chinese shops. In the windows you can see the chefs cooking the food.

Brick Lane

There are more Indian restaurants than fish and chip shops in London. If you want to eat an Indian curry, the best place is Brick Lane. Brick Lane is in Whitechapel, East London. The most popular dish is chicken tikka masala.

Restaurant names

Here are 8 restaurants you can find in London. Look at the signs. What type of food do you think they sell?

French • Japanese • Italian • American • Chinese • English • Indian • Chinese

Planet Hollywood	1	Wok Wok	5 ....
Masala Zone	2	The Chippy	6 ....
Yo! Sushi	3	Café Rouge	7 ....
Pizza Express	4	Noodle Time	8 ....

At the restaurant

Answer these questions. The correct answers give you the different ingredients* of a popular dish. What is the dish?

1 You are looking for a table. You see a table. It's got the sign "Reserved" on it. Do you...
- sit at the table? ➤ rice
- look for another table? ➤ fish

2 When you get the bill, it says "Service not included". This means...
- you must wash up ➤ chicken
- you must leave some extra money for the waiter ➤ chips

3 You want to pay. What do you ask for?
- The bill ➤ vinegar
- The ben ➤ tomato sauce

What dish is it?

....

Who says it?

You are in a restaurant. Who says these phrases, the waiter or the customer? Write W or C next to the correct phrases.

Ready to order?	☐	Table for two, please.	☐
I'm a vegetarian.	☐	I'd like to pay, please.	☐
I'm allergic* to nuts.	☐	Where would you like to sit?	☐
Would you like some pepper?	☐	Can I have another fork?	☐
Would you like anything to drink?	☐	I'd like the green salad.	☐

Choose a restaurant from the list above. Find a partner to be the waiter and make a dialogue together.

VOCABULARY CHECK LIST

What is it in your language? Find out!

- far ☐
- pie ☐
- eels ☐
- vinegar ☐
- to wrap ☐
- takeaway ☐
- ingredients ☐
- allergic ☐

www.londoneats.com

Everyday Londoners

London is the biggest city in Europe and the 20th biggest city in the world.

London's population*

Over the centuries, people from all over the world have come to London. They came to find freedom, to find work, to meet people and live an interesting life. They make London an exciting and diverse* city.

Today, more than seven million people live in London and 46% of these are under 35 years old.

Look at this pie chart. It shows the different ethnic groups that make London so cosmopolitan*.

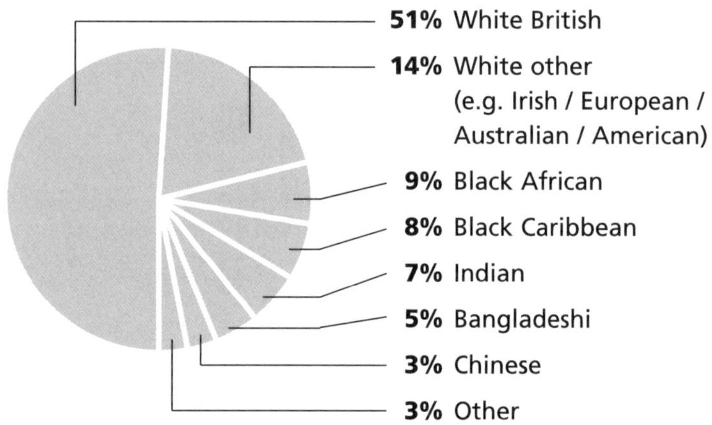

Get into groups to discuss these questions:

- What's the population of your town / city?
- What ethnic groups are in your city / town?
- What are the difficulties for people from different cultures / ethnic groups living in London?

Writing home

Imagine you arrive to live in London to start a new life.
You go to the Internet café to write home. Complete the e-mail with your own ideas.

Dear ....

How are you? I arrived in London on Tuesday.

I'm living in .... (*a flat / house / bedsit**)

in .... (*area in London*)

The most difficult thing about living in London is ....

....

The best thing about living in London is ....

....

Hope you are all well. I will call you next week.

Love ....

London's workers

If you go to London on a weekday and look around, most people you see are wearing suits*. This is because 42% of Londoners work in offices and businesses. The average* Londoner earns £600 a week. That's about £200 more than people in other places in England.

Where do most people work in your city?

....

....

Calling for a job

It's easy to find work in London, especially if you want a summer or a part-time job. But telephoning for a job is not always so easy. Gianni is looking for a job, but he doesn't use the correct style of English.

Match what his wrong way of saying things to the right way of saying things.

Waiter / Waitress needed for pizza restaurant in central London.

Experience* preferred*. Good pay.
Call Stephen Briggs 0207 421 9052
100-102 Conduit Street, London

1. Hi Steve, I'm Gianni.
2. I was looking in the newspaper the other day and I saw your job for a waiter. It sounds pretty cool. Is the job still going?
3. Cool. So what's it like then? What are the hours of work like? I hope I don't have to work late. What's the pay like? I have to know about the money!
4. Yeah. I've done a bit of waiting before in Italy. In the summer, I think. I'm Italian, so what more could you want?
5. Sure. I'll drop in on Tuesday at three. See ya!

a) Great. Could you give me a few details* about the job?

b) Of course. I'll come to the interview on Tuesday at three o'clock. Thank you very much. Good bye.

c) Good afternoon. Am I speaking to Mr Briggs? My name is Gianni Rossi.

d) I'm calling about the vacancy* in Monday's *Evening Standard.* Are you still looking for somebody?

e) Yes I have got some experience of waiting. Last summer I worked in a small restaurant in my home town of Pisa, so I know how to wait and I know Italian food!

We can't read what Mr Briggs says to Gianni. What do you think he says?

VOCABULARY CHECK LIST **What is it in your language? Find out!**

population	cosmopolitan	suits	experience	detail
diverse	bedsit	average	to prefer	vacancy

www.netlondon.com/employment/job-hunting

The Boat Race

Every country has got its own strange historic sport or race such as the Palio in Sienna, Italy, or the Pamplona Bull Run in Spain, but the Boat Race in London is one of the most extraordinary to understand. It is simply a race between two boats, one from Oxford University and one from Cambridge University. 2004 is special because it's the year of the 150th Boat Race.

History

The first race was in 1829 in Henley, a small town on the Thames. 20,000 people watched it and now Henley is famous for its annual regatta – a series of boat races in July each year. People come dressed in fashionable clothes and have expensive, luxurious* picnics on the River during the races. After the first year, the Boat Race moved to Westminster, but by 1845 when Westminster became too crowded*, the Race moved six miles (9.65 km) up the River Thames to Putney which was only a village in those days but it's a fashionable suburb of London now.

Facts

The two long boats measure 19.9 metres and they are very light – they only weigh 96 kg. The race lasts for 6.8 km. It takes approximately* 600 strokes (a movement of the oars of the boat) to row the course. There are eight oarsmen (people who row the boat) in each boat and a cox (short for *coxswain* – the person who steers* the boat). The oarsmen are big and strong but the cox is always a very small person. Every crew* member has to train for two hours for each stroke (one movement of the oar) – that's 1,200 hours! That's a lot of training!

The Race takes place at Easter time, and the water in the River Thames between Putney and Mortlake is very tidal*. The streams of water move very fast when the tide is coming up the Thames. The weather, the tide, and the bends in the River mean that the difficult parts of the River are exposed* to winds from different directions and this adds mystery to the unpredictable* conditions.

The Spectators

400 million people in the world watch the Boat Race on TV, and 7.7 million people in Britain watch it. The Boat Race is in the top five live* TV sports events on British TV.

VOCABULARY CHECK LIST

What is it in your language? Find out!

luxurious ______

crowded ______

approximately ______

to steer ______

crew ______

tidal ______

exposed ______

unpredictable ______

live (adj) ______

www.theboatrace.org

Boat Race Statistics

Like all famous sports, there are lots of statistics connected with it. Fill in the missing words in these sentences and then find them in the word search grid. Draw red lines through them all when you find them. The extra words in the grid (not coloured red) spell the name of the oldest person to take part in the Boat Race, and they also tell you what happened in 1912.

1. The ....*fastest*.......... time for the Boat Race is 16 minutes, 19 seconds. Cambridge did this in 1998.
2. Christopher Hibbert was the .... oarsman to row in the Boat Race. He weighed 110.22 kg.
3. Alfred Higgins was the .... oarsman to row in the Boat Race. He weighed 60.1kg. He took part in 1882. But there were two tiny coxes who took part in 1862 and 1939. Francis Archer (Cambridge) and Hart Massey (Oxford) both weighed just 32.66 kg.
4. Matthew Brittin (Cambridge) was the .... person to take part in the Boat Race. He was just eighteen years old in 1987.
5. The .... winning margin (the distance between the two boats at the finish) was just 0.3048m. This was in 2003. It was a very exciting race!
6. The .... oarsman rowed for Cambridge. He took part four times in the Boat Race: in 1999, 2000, 2001 and 2002. He measured 2m 7cm.
7. In 1981, Sue Brown (Oxford) was the first .... to take part in the Boat Race.
8. The .... twins rowed in the Boat Race in 1982.
9. In 1989, both Oxford and Cambridge had .... coxes.

~~F~~	~~A~~	~~S~~	~~T~~	~~E~~	~~S~~	~~T~~	L	T
E	A	N	S	D	S	S	I	S
M	Y	P	E	E	R	E	G	E
A	O	B	L	E	R	G	H	I
L	T	L	L			N	T	V
E	A	S	A	A	N	U	E	A
T	N	A	M	O	W	O	S	E
F	I	R	S	T	K	Y	T	H

The oldest person to take part in the Boat Race was

☐☐☐☐ ☐☐☐☐☐☐☐.

He was the Cambridge cox in 1992 when he was 38 years old.

In 1912, the two boats ☐☐☐☐.

Wimbledon: The Home of Tennis

When people hear the word Wimbledon they think of one thing – tennis.

Wimbledon in south-west London is a pretty, quiet place. But for two weeks in the summer it's really busy. Wimbledon is the home of one of the most important tennis championships* in the world.

In the last week of June and the first week of July, more than half a million people come to Wimbledon to see the world's best tennis players.

After two weeks, with more than one hundred matches and 15,000 tennis balls, you have two tennis champions!

Wimbledon is more than just tennis. Here are five things you can see at Wimbledon!

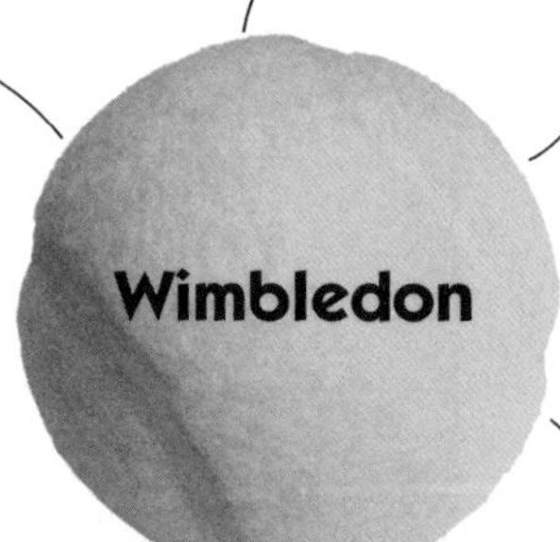

1 Strawberries

If you visit Wimbledon you must have strawberries and cream. They are expensive but it is the tradition!

2 Pimms

The traditional summer drink is Pimms (an alcoholic drink) and lemonade.

3 Clothes

The tennis players have a dress code* (they must wear white).

4 Tents

Yes, at Wimbledon it's possible to buy tickets on the same day, but there are not many and the first people in the queue* get the tickets. That's why some people camp the night before so they are the first in the queue!

5 Umbrellas

It may be the summer but it is traditional for it to rain at some time during Wimbledon so you must take an umbrella!

Wimbledon rules

You are playing at Wimbledon. You are serving*. Read the sentences below and chose the correct answer. Find that answer in the tennis balls and see how many serves you get.

1 Players *must / mustn't* wear white.
2 You *must / mustn't* take photos during a match.
3 You *mustn't / must* buy a ticket before the match.
4 You *must / mustn't* talk during a match.
5 Lots of people drink Pimms at Wimbledon. But you *must / mustn't* drink it if you are under 18.

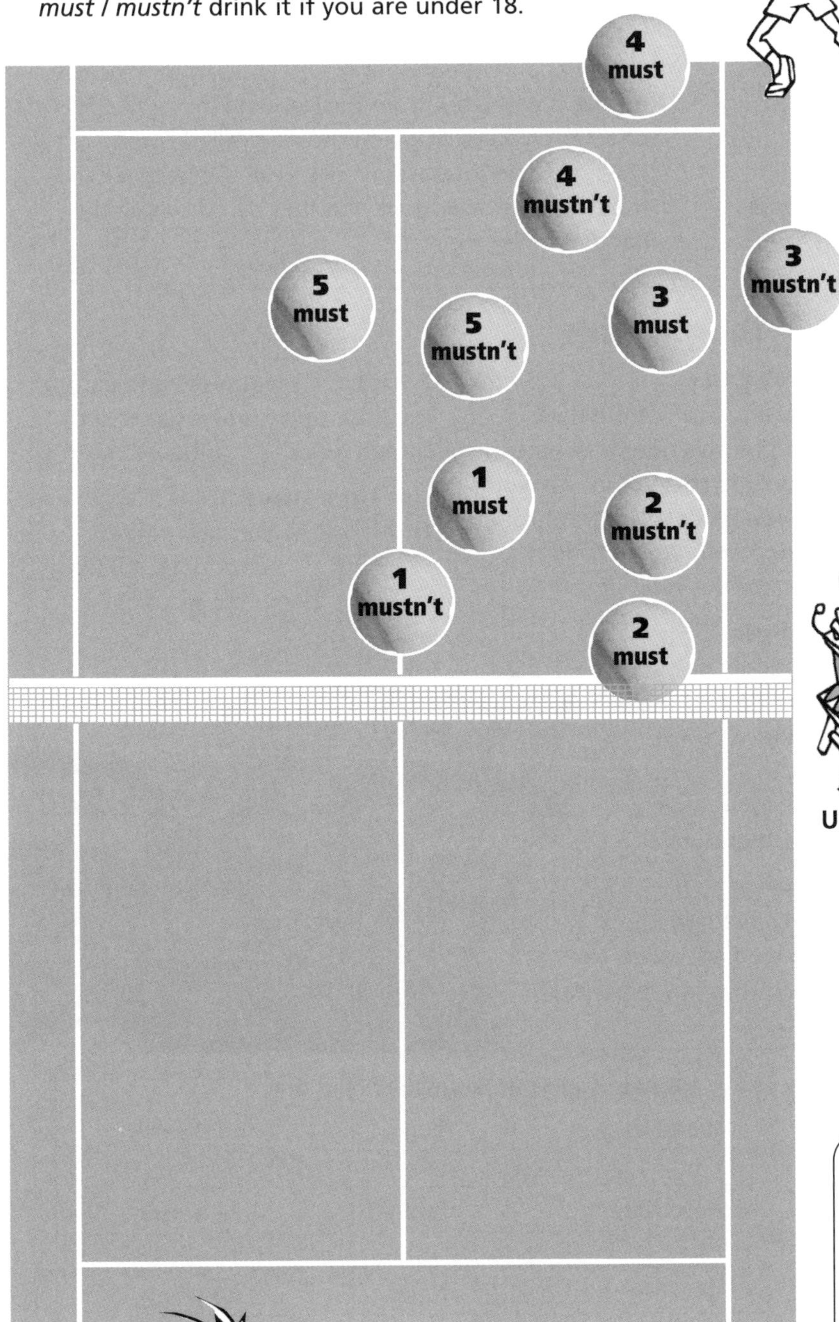

Tennis talk!

Are you a tennis expert? You hear people talking in the crowd. What do they mean?

1 ACE *a*

"Wow! Roddick hits another ace!"

a) Roddick serves. The other player can't touch the ball. Roddick scores a point.

b) Roddick hits the tennis ball into the net.

2 LOVE

"Oh no! Tim is losing two games to love."

a) Tim is in love and can't play very well.

b) Tim has no points.

3 SEED

"That player is one of the seeds."

a) The player is one of the best in the world.

b) The player is one of the worst in the world.

VOCABULARY CHECK LIST

What is it in your language? Find out!

championship	queue
dress code	**to serve**

www.wimbledon.org/en_GB/index.html

Theme Parks Around London

If you love adventure, you must visit some of the theme parks near London.

Chessington World of Adventures

If you want to go to Chessington, you must get a train from Waterloo Station. Chessington is south west of London in a county called Surrey. There are lots of scary* rides*. They measure you for some of the rides. Small children mustn't go on any of the dangerous rides (The Vampire, The Samurai, Dragon Falls, the Black Bucaneer and the Seastorm). Also, very fat people can't go on some of the rides because it's difficult to close the safety bars* on the seats if you are too big.

One part of Chessington is called Animal Land. It hasn't got any rides, but it's got a zoo with some wonderful animals. There is a gorilla family with Kumba and Kaya (the mum and dad), their daughter Asili, and Asili's daughter, Shani. There is also a big sea lion called Boris. He weighs 1,764kg! He's too heavy for all the rides but he can hear all the screams*!

If you love Harry Potter, wizards* and magic, there's a scary house called Hocus Pocus Hall. If you don't like scary things, you can go on the Skyway Safari. This is a slow and gentle monorail and you can look down on the theme park from the sky. And if you like lots of action, you must go on the ride called Tomb Blaster. It's an interactive* ride – all the people on the ride have laser guns and they can shoot all the baddies* they meet.

Thorpe Park

Thorpe Park is in the west of London, near Heathrow Airport. It's got lots of very scary rides. Here are some of them:

Nemesis Inferno
This rollercoaster* goes upside down. It's a journey* through a volcano and you travel at 77km/h.

Colossus
This rollercoaster climbs to 30m then falls to the ground and goes up into the sky like a rocket. It goes into a 360° loop*. It twists* through the air over the water and does 10 loops during the ride. 1050 people go on this ride every hour. Some brave people go on it again and again!

X:\No Way Out
If you are afraid* of the dark, don't go on this ride! It's one of the first rollercoasters in the world where you go backwards* through the dark. There are no little children on this ride!

The Eclipse
Some people prefer* a quiet ride and this is like the Safari Skyway in Chessington. You can look down on all the other rides.

The Vortex
This very fast ride is in a part of the Park called The Lost City. This ride swings* 20m above the ground and each of the little cages rotate (go round) fifteen times.

The Tidal Wave
This is one of Europe's highest water rides. It lasts 136 seconds.

VOCABULARY CHECK LIST What is it in your language? Find out!

scary	scream	baddies	loop	backwards
ride	wizard	rollercoaster	to twist	to prefer
safety bar	interactive	journey	afraid	to swing

www.chessington.co.uk www.thorpepark.co.uk

Both these parks are closed October-March.

The Tomb Blaster Puzzle

If you go to Chessington World of Adventures, where can you find the Tomb Blaster ride? Choose the letters next to the correct parts of the sentences and you can find the name of that part of the theme park.

Early in the morning at Chessington there are only **1** ...*a few*... **(some – L / a few – I)** visitors because **2** .... **(lots – D / some – E)** of people come to the Park by coach. There are **3** .... **(a few – A / no – O)** pandas in Animal Land but there are **4** .... **(any – M / a few – R)** gorillas and **5** .... **(some – P / lots – E)** of penguins. There are **6** .... **(no – N / any – A)** elephants. **7** .... **(A few – S / Lots – D)** of people work in Animal Land because the animals are very hungry in the morning. **8** .... **(No – W / Some – N)** people don't like scary rides but there are **9** .... **(lots – T / a few – B)** of things for them to do. **10** .... **(No – S / Some – I)** people dress in cowboy clothes for a funny photograph; others go on the monorail trip. **11** .... **(Any – C / No – O)** visit is complete without a meal in one of the themed restaurants. **12** .... **(A few – M / Any – N)** people love rollercoasters so much that they go on the Vampire five or six times but it's difficult because there are always **13** .... **(a few – D / lots – B)** of people in the queue. If you have **14** .... **(no – T / any – E)** doubts, don't go because it's really frightening! Have you got **15** .... **(any – G / some – J)** favourite rides from theme parks in your country? **16** .... **(Any – Y / Some – H)** small children hate the dodgems because they can easily bump their heads when the cars crash into one another. In Beanoland at Chessington there are **17** .... **(a few – H / lots – F)** of rides with names of characters from the comic, *The Beano*, such as Dennis's Madhouse. Dennis the Menace is a naughty boy in *The Beano*. He's got a dog called Gnasher. Do **18** .... **(a few – A / any – K)** of you know *The Beano*? One thing is sure, if you come to Chessington, you are going to have **19** .... **(lots – D / no – F)** of fun.

								i										
9	**16**	**5**	**17**	**11**	**4**	**13**	**1**	**19**	**2**	**14**	**8**	**18**	**10**	**6**	**15**	**7**	**3**	**12**

Five Stars

At many theme parks there are some stars next to the names of the rides to warn you how scary they are. X:\No Way Out has got five stars. Some other rides have four stars, some have three, some have two and some have one star.

Here are the different meanings of the stars. Choose one, two, three, four or five stars for each of them.

Thrilling	
For little children	
Extreme	
Fun for the family	
Intense	

City Animals

There are more than 7 million people in London, and where there are people, there are animals. Here are the most common animals you will see in London.

Name: Fox

Eats:
Small animals, insects; loves 'fast food' (eg hamburgers and chips)

How many?
There are 30,000 in London! A fox even lives in Downing Street!

Pawprint:

Fact:
Foxes have a white tip* on their tails

Foxes live in my town / city ☐

Name: Pigeon

Eats:
Insects, nuts, bread, chips

How many?
40,000 pigeons fly into Trafalgar Square every day

Footprint:

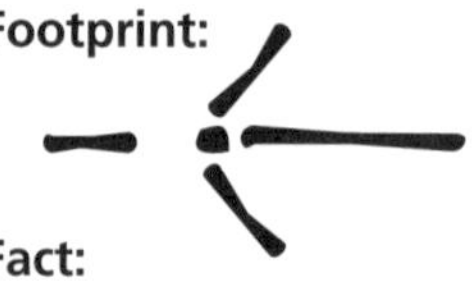

Fact:
Pigeons can live for 35 years

Pigeons live in my town / city ☐

Name: Rat

Eats:
Insects, fast food, rubbish

How many?
There are 60 million in the UK

Fact:
There are more rats than people in London

Pawprint:

Rats live in my town / city ☐

Pests!

Pigeons, foxes and rats are pests* that damage* buildings and spread disease*.

The Mayor of London wants to reduce* the number of pigeons and rats in London. For example, it is now against the law to feed the pigeons in Trafalgar Square.

Here are six ideas to reduce the number of pigeons, foxes and rats. What's your opinion? 1 = the best idea 6 = the worst idea

- ☐ Put more litter bins in the city
- ☐ Put poison* in the streets to kill the animals
- ☐ Put traps* in the streets to kill the animals
- ☐ Encourage people to have cats
- ☐ Fine* people who drop litter on the street
- ☐ Make fast food shops pay a 'pest tax'

Who are the real pests – people or animals?

VOCABULARY CHECK LIST **What is it in your language? Find out!**

tip	to damage	to reduce	trap
pest	to spread disease	poison	to fine

www.wildlondon.org.uk/wildinfo/foxes.htm

The London Aquarium

Fill in the missing words in the text to find a fascinating fact about sharks. The words in (boxes) make the fact sentence.

fish (U.S.) like (BY) eating (KILLED) sleep (ARE) facts (THE) weapon (SHARKS)
shark (IN) strange (BEES) males (THAN) ~~floors (MORE)~~ temperature (PEOPLE)

The London Aquarium is opposite the Houses of Parliament, on the bank of the River Thames. In the different areas of the Aquarium you can see fish from the different oceans of the world.

The Sharks

In the Pacific area you can see the sharks and sting rays. You can look at them from two ....floors.... (MORE) of the Aquarium because they need very deep water. The .... (   ) of the water must always be 23°. There are three sand tiger sharks, three brown sharks, a nurse shark called Florence and Mazawabee, a zebra .... (   ). You can learn lots of interesting .... (   ) about sharks at the London Aquarium. Sharks are the only .... (   ) with eyelids* but they can .... (   ) with their eyes open. Great white sharks love .... (   ) but they don't chew their food. They rip* their food into chunks* and swallow them whole. Tiger sharks can be dangerous because they .... (   ) biting people but the good news is they don't like the taste and they usually stop after one bite. Sharks are heavier than water and they can easily sink if they stop swimming.

The Indian Ocean

The Indian Ocean is the world's third largest ocean. It contains some of the world's most dangerous fish too. Starfish are very .... (   ) creatures. They can easily push their stomachs up through their mouths when they want to eat. Bleeaagghh!

Unusual Fish

On a coral reef* you can see lion fish, eels, bat fish, pipe fish and sea horses. These unusual fish can swim upright, and the .... (   ), not the females, give birth to the babies. The box fish can easily protect itself when it's in danger. Its secret .... (   ) is poison. It squirts* poison into the water when danger approaches, but it has to swim away quickly because it can poison itself, too!

The electric knife fish which lives in Venezuela has got tiny eyes and it can hardly* see. It uses electricity to hunt for food.

Puffer fish can puff* themselves up angrily when they are in danger. Atlantic puffer fish have got lots of spikes* on their bodies.

VOCABULARY CHECK LIST
What is it in your language? Find out!

eyelid
(   )
to rip
(   )
chunk
(   )
coral reef
(   )
to squirt
(   )
hardly
(   )
to puff
(   )
spike
(   )

FACT: ....More..

....

www.londonaquarium.co.uk

London Zoo

London Zoo is in Regent's Park near the centre of London. It's open every day of the year except Christmas Day. There are 600 different species (kinds) of animals, birds, insects and reptiles there. It has changed a lot since it first opened in 1828, and although many people now think it's cruel to keep animals in zoos, it's a good place to protect* animals in danger and to educate people, especially children, about the natural world. Some of the animals became living legends in their lifetimes.

Guy the Gorilla

Guy got his name from the day when he was born – Guy Fawkes Day (November 5th). He was born in 1947 and arrived at the zoo holding a little metal* hot water bottle. He was very gentle and everyone loved him. When sparrows* flew into his enclosure (the space where he lived), he picked them up* gently in his hand, looked at them closely, and then let them fly away. Signs everywhere told the visitors not to feed the animals, but people gave Guy sweets and he got toothache. He died during an operation* to remove his tooth. There's a statue of Guy at London Zoo.

Belinda, the Bird-eating Spider

Belinda died in 1993 when she was 23 years old. She was a great advert* for London Zoo because she helped hundreds of people conquer* their spider phobia. The zoo allowed people to hold beautiful Belinda in their hands and usually this cured them.

Winnie, the Black Bear

Winnie arrived at the zoo in 1914. A. A. Milne, the children's writer, took his young son, Christopher Robin, to the zoo and he began to make up stories about the bear. These were the first stories about Winnie-the-Pooh.

Goldie, the Golden Eagle

Goldie escaped in 1965 and thousands of people went to Regent's Park to watch him flying from tree to tree. It caused big traffic jams* around the area near the Park. He was free for eleven days and he became a national hero.

VOCABULARY CHECK LIST
What is it in your language? Find out!

to protect ______

metal ______

sparrow ______

to pick up ______

operation ______

advert ______

to conquer ______

traffic jams ______

www.londonzoo.co.uk

The Zoo Maze

This is the story of London Zoo. Choose the correct verb to complete each sentence. Take the letters next to the correct verbs to find the popular name for some of the Zoo's favourite animals, the okapi.

START

The Regent's Park Zoo opened in 1828 but ordinary people *couldn't* visit it until 1847.

F WOULDN'T

A herd of sheep and goats .... from London docks to the zoo with the new African animals to provide milk to feed them.

G WALKED

In 1850 the first hippopotamus (since Roman times) arrived. The number of visitors to the Zoo ....

J COULDN'T

E TRANSLATED

N ARRIVED

A SAILED

S TWICED

L DOUBLED

In 1832 zoo keepers .... an elephant, an alligator, a boa, an anaconda and 100 rattlesnakes from the Tower of London.

U TRANSFERRED

Tommy, the first chimpanzee, ... at the Zoo in a stagecoach with his keeper.

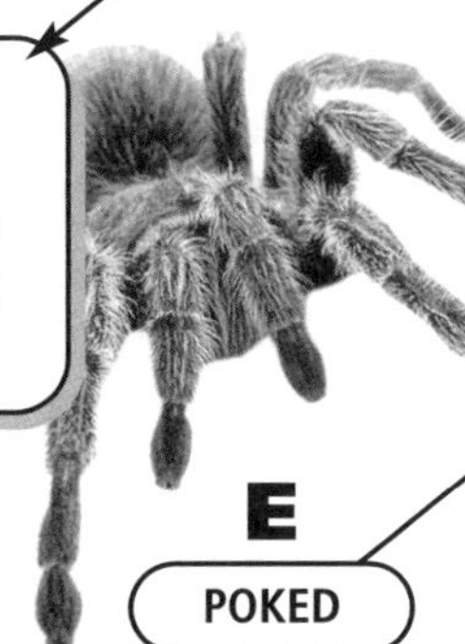

In the late 1840s, excited Victorian women .... their parasols through the bars of the cages to try to touch the animals.

C CLOSED

B DYED

W WENT

E POKED

M PULLED

In 1853, the world's first reptile house ....

G DIED

The first lion .... of a broken heart in 1840 after the death of his mate.

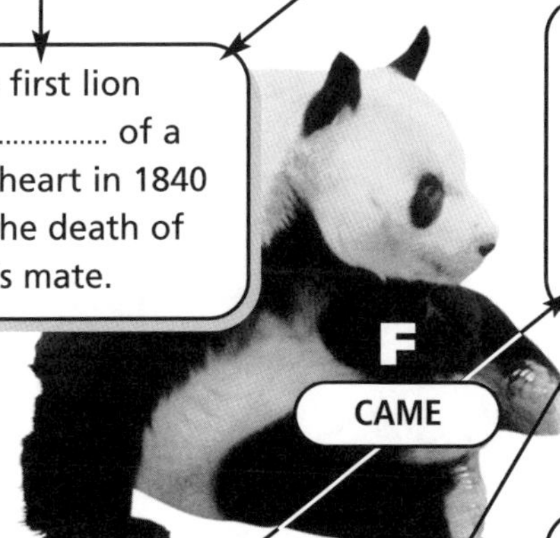

During World War II, keepers .... the dangerous animals to Ireland for safety and people ate the edible fish.

I OPENED

D KISSED

F CAME

E TOOK

A keeper tried to charm the cobra, but it .... him between the eyes and he died.

T ESCAPED

The first koala bear to live outside Australia .... to the Zoo in 1880.

G BROUGHT

After the War, London Zoo .... their first giant panda and their first polar bear.

R BIT

Y EAT

F HURRIED

R BREAD

S BRED

A giant ant eater also arrived in the 1850s. It .... 50 eggs a day.

A ATE

Everyone .... to see Alice and Jumbo, the two new elephants who arrived in 1867.

I WORRIED

FINISH

EastEnders

Londoners have got lots of places they can go to and lots of things they can do but sometimes they just like to stay at home and watch television.

Britain's favourite soap opera is set in the East End of London. It's called *EastEnders* and it's about people who live in the East End of London. It's on BBC1 and its the most popular TV show in the UK – more than 15 million people watch it. You can watch *EastEnders* four times a week on Mondays, Tuesdays, Thursdays and Fridays – and if you miss an episode* you can watch all the week's episodes on Sunday afternoon.

The EastEnders live in Albert Square, Walford. Walford is not a real place in London. Here is a map of Walford. Label the nine places.

1 The 'Queen Vic' pub
2 A laundrette
3 A market stall
4 The café
5 Walford East Underground Station
6 Angie's Den (a nightclub)
7 Evans & Son Cars
8 The Arches motor repairs
9 The Bed and Breakfast

There are 30 – 35 characters in EastEnders. Here are some of the favourites:

Alfie Moon

Alfie lives and works in the pub. He is in love with Kat but he is very shy.

Kat Slater

Kat works in the pub. She gets angry very quickly. She often falls in love with the wrong men.

Phil Mitchell

Many people are afraid of Phil. He owns the car repair* shop, the café and the pub. People say he is horrible and arrogant* but he loves his baby daughter.

Janine

Janine likes money... and trouble. She often uses people for money. She works for Evans' Cars.

Jim Branning

Jim is married to Dot. He works in the pub. He likes to drink and gamble*, but only if Dot doesn't know!

Dot Cotton

Dot is married to Jim. She is always smoking and loves talking about other people. She works in the laundrette*.

Make your own EastEnders episode

You need a dice for this activity. Get into groups and decide which character you want to be. Roll the dice to give you a place, a situation, a phrase and a prop*.

You then have ten minutes to decide what happens and make a dialogue. At the end you can act it to your class or roll the dice again. To finish the activity, write up your dialogue as a script.

Dice number	Places	Situation	Prop	Say it!
1	The 'Queen Vic' pub	There's a birthday	A bag	Come on!
2	The laundrette	There's a wedding	A mobile phone	Get lost!
3	The market stall	One of you needs money	An address book	Shut up!
4	The café	There's an accident	Some keys	Alright, mate?
5	Walford East underground station	One of you has got an exam / test	A pair of scissors	No way!
6	Evans and Son Cars	One of you is in love with two people	A train ticket	You're joking!

VOCABULARY CHECK LIST

What is it in your language? Find out!

episode ______

repair ______

arrogant ______

to gamble ______

laundrette ______

prop ______

www.bbc.co.uk/eastenders

The London Marathon

If you see thousands of people running in London in April it can only be one event* – The London Marathon*!

Every year, in the second week of April, more than 35,000 people come to London to run in the London Marathon. The Marathon is 26 miles (42km). It's not only for professional sports people – anybody can run in the Marathon. The oldest person to run in the London Marathon was 91 years old and the youngest was 18. If you are under 18 years old, you can run in the mini-Marathon. Many people run in costumes and collect money for charity*. One year, a couple got married* in the race too!

True (T) or False (F)?
Use the text above to help you.

1. The Marathon is held twice a year.
   F – It's held every year.
2. Only Londoners can enter the London Marathon.
3. You can run in the London Marathon at any age.
4. You don't have to be a professional sports person to run in the Marathon.
5. Professional sports people often run in costumes.
6. The mini-Marathon is for children and teenagers.

Work in pairs. Discuss.

Is there a Marathon in your country? If so, when is it and where?

Would you prefer to watch the Marathon or run in it? Give reasons.

Are you fit enough for the Marathon?

Answer the questions about your daily life to find out how far you can run in the London Marathon.

1 When do you get up?
a) I get up before 7 o'clock. ☐
b) Late! I get up ten minutes before school starts. ☐

2 What do you have for breakfast?
a) I don't have time for breakfast. I have a bar of chocolate at eleven o'clock. ☐
b) Eggs, muesli and a glass of orange juice or milk. ☐

3 How do you travel to school?
a) I go by bike or on foot. ☐
b) I go by bus, train or car. ☐

4 What do you do in your free time?
a) I sit in front of my TV or computer. ☐
b) I don't have any free time, I am always busy. ☐

5 How often do you run?
a) Only when I am late for the bus. ☐
b) All the time, when I'm doing sport. ☐

6 How many press-ups* can you do?
a) One to ten. ☐
b) More than ten. ☐

7 When it's time for sports at school, what do you do?
a) I pretend* to be sick. ☐
b) I stay for extra practice. ☐

8 When do you go to bed?
a) Before 10.30pm. ☐
b) After 10.30pm. I'm usually at a party or on the computer. ☐

Now look at the answers:

1	**a)** 3 miles	**b)** 1mile	**5**	**a)** 1 mile	**b)** 3 miles
2	**a)** 1 mile	**b)** 3 miles	**6**	**a)** 1 mile	**b)** 5 miles
3	**a)** 3 miles	**b)** 1 mile	**7**	**a)** 0 mile	**b)** 3 miles
4	**a)** 0 miles	**b)** 4 miles	**8**	**a)** 2 miles	**b)** 0 miles

Total miles = ...

Now see how far you run in the London Marathon!

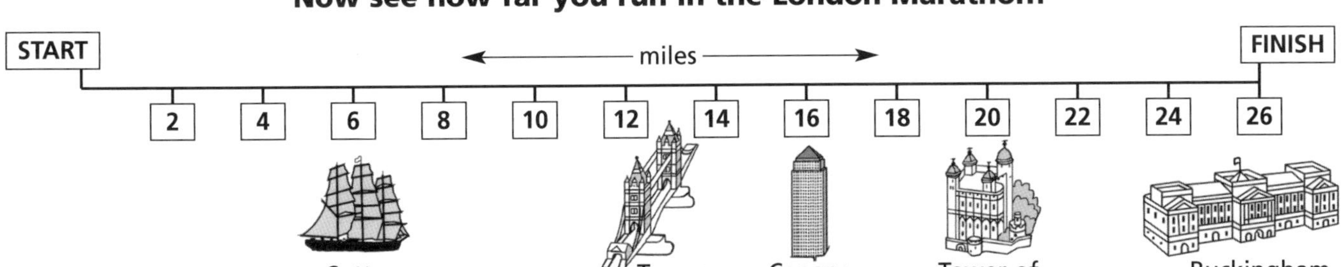

VOCABULARY CHECK LIST
What is it in your language? Find out!

event	charity	press-ups
Marathon	to get married	to pretend

www.london-marathon.co.uk

Notting Hill and the Carnival

Welcome to Europe's biggest street festival – The Notting Hill Carnival!

August is carnival time in London. In Notting Hill, West London, there is a big party for two days in August. Nearly two million people come to look at the costumes, listen to the music and dance in the streets.

The costumes

It takes a long time to make a costume for the carnival, sometimes a year! Some of the costumes have got 200,000 sequins* on them. The best costumes win a prize*.

What costume are you going to wear?

....

....

The food

The traditional food at the carnival is Caribbean. There are 300 food stalls* and every year people eat 16,000 coconuts and a tonne of chicken!

You can try one of these dishes.
What are you going to eat?

Saltfish fritters* ☐
Curried* goat* ☐
Coconut ☐

The music

The carnival is noisy! There are 40 sound systems*. They play more than 30,000 records during the carnival!

You are a DJ at a street party.
What records are you going to play?

....

....

....

Party people

Here are five people who are at the carnival. What's going to happen? Use the verbs in the box to make *going to* sentences.

to get sunburn • to have a headache
to be sick • ~~to win the costume competition~~
to steal a mobile phone

1 *She's going to win the costume competition.*

2

3

4

5

Notting Hill carnival route

Look at the map.

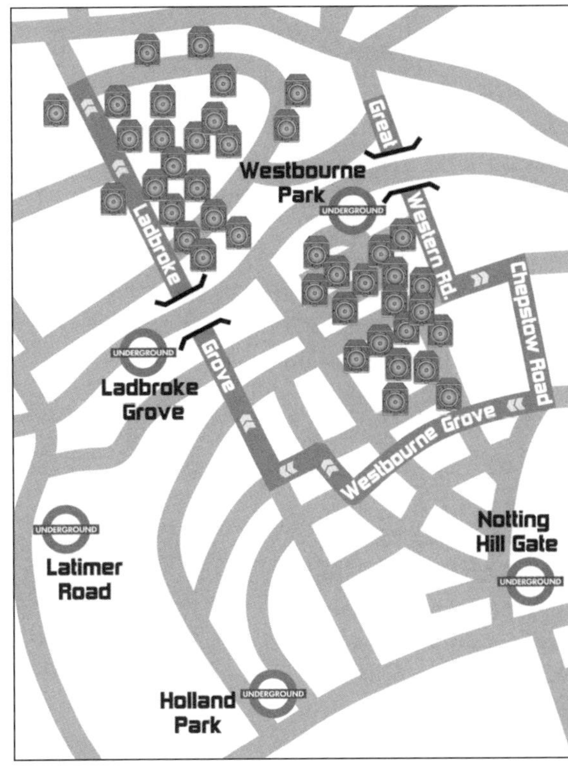

How many underground stations can you find?

+

How many sound systems can you find?

÷

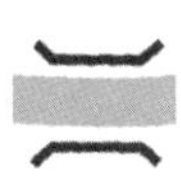

How many bridges can you find?

=

Do the sum. This tells you the date of the Notting Hill carnival.

It's on August

VOCABULARY CHECK LIST

What is it in your language? Find out!

sequin	fritter
prize	curried goat
stalls	sound system

www.portowebbo.co.uk/nottinghilltv/carnival.htm

Leicester Square: London Cinemas

22 million people visit Leicester (*pronounced 'Lester'*) Square every year. It's near Piccadilly Circus and there are several big cinemas in the square itself plus lots more nearby.

You can go to Leicester Square when there's a première* of a big new film and you will see plenty of famous film stars walking along the red carpet* to the cinema. You'll see lots of photographers and you might even pick up* a bit of celebrity* gossip*.

Film Certificates

It's a bit scary – so are you allowed to see it? Each film has a special 'certificate' which means only certain people are allowed to see it. Match the certificates to the definitions:

- U certificate
- PG certificate
- 12A certificate
- 15 certificate
- 18 certificate

a) You are not allowed to see it if you are younger than fifteen

b) You are not allowed to see it if you are younger than eighteen

c) Everyone is allowed to see it

d) Children under twelve are not allowed to see it unless they are accompanied by an adult

e) Children under twelve are allowed to see it if their parents think it's OK

Here are some famous British actors. Take the two letters after their names and put them in the correct order to discover the title of a successful British film.

Daniel Radcliffe (VE)

Kate Winslet (TU)

Pierce Brosnan (AC)

Orlando Bloom (AL)

Ewan McGregor (LO)

Hugh Grant (LY)

Which British actor…

… has been in a few *Star Wars* films?

Ewan McGregor .... (LO)

… has spent a great deal of time in Hogwarts School?

.... (   )

… has got lots female fans because his name is "Bond, James Bond"?

.... (   )

… had a few scary moments in cold water with Leo DiCaprio?

.... (   )

… wore a couple of pointed ears in three very successful films?

.... (   )

… has had plenty of experience of playing a shy, aristocratic Englishman?

.... (   )

The name of the film is: LO..

VOCABULARY CHECK LIST

What is it in your language? Find out!

première

carpet

to pick up

celebrity

gossip

http://movies.yahoo.com/upcoming

Music in London

**London is a great place to hear live music.
These famous British pop stars are all singing about the future in their hit songs.
Fill in the missing words, and take the correct letter to spell the name of
London's most popular rock concert venue. Choose from these words:**

YOU • IMPOSSIBLE • MAYBE • SAVES • HEART
DREAM • WITH • MAN • I'LL • FEED • ~~STRONG~~ • AT

1 Though the sea will be ....STRONG....
I know we'll carry on, 'cos if there's somebody calling
me on; she's the one.
(third letter = ...R....)
She's the One (Robbie Williams)

2 Give me just a second and I'll be alright
Surely one more moment
couldn't break my ....
(second letter = ...)
Gotta Get Thru This (Daniel Bedingfield)

3 Will you still need me,
will you still .... me
When I'm sixty-four?
(third letter = ...)
When I'm Sixty-four (The Beatles)

4 I'm flying high,
like the wind, reaching the .... ;
I'll never doubt again.
(tenth letter = ...)
Anything is Possible (Gareth Gates)

5 And I think it's going to be a long, long time
Till touchdown* brings me round again to find
I'm not the .... they think I am at home.
(third letter = ...)
Rocket Man (Elton John)

6 You'll always be the .... that fills my head
(fifth letter = ...)
Never had a Dream Come True (S Club 7)

7 Wanna take my time for me, all me
So .... tomorrow I'll find my way home.
(fourth letter = ...)
Maybe Tomorrow (Stereophonics)

8 Look .... the stars,
look how they shine for you
And all the things that you do.
(first letter = ...)
Yellow (Coldplay)

9 Well, I won't go down .... this ship
And I won't put up my hands and surrender*
(first letter = ...)
White Flag (Dido)

10 Every bond* you break,
Every step you take,
I'll be watching ....
(first letter = ...)
Every Breath You Take (Sting)

11 You're gonna be the one who .... me
And after all, you're my wonder wall.
(second letter = ...)
Wonderwall (Oasis)

12 For now .... have to wait,
But baby, if you change your mind, don't be late,
(third letter = ...)
Whole Again (Atomic Kitten)

9	3	6	7	12	2	10

	R			
8	1	4	5	11

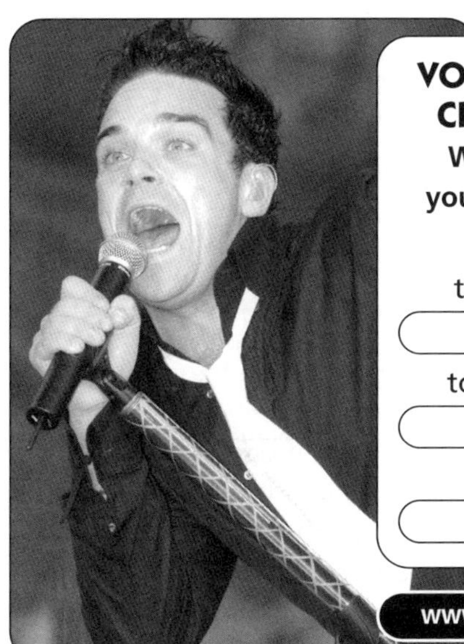

VOCABULARY CHECK LIST
What is it in your language? Find out!

touchdown
to surrender
bond

www.poplyrics.net

Party in the Park

Every July, 100,000 people go to Hyde Park in London for the Party in the Park. Pop stars from all over the world take part in a concert to raise money for the Prince's Trust. In 2003 the Party in the Park raised £1 million, but the Prince's Trust needs to raise £53 million every year. Why? And what is it?

The Princes's Trust

It's been running since 1976. The 'prince' in the title is Prince Charles. He realised that many young people (aged 14 – 30) were not rich enough or skilful* enough to reach their full potential* in life. Some of them came from poor homes and weren't rich enough to go to university. Others had been in trouble* with the police or simply had not been lucky enough to have chances to develop their skills. The Trust helps young people to get training and experience*. It's got special links with sport, music and fashion, and it organises workshops to give disadvantaged* young people some useful experience. If some of the young people who join the projects are ambitious enough, they can sometimes get help from the Prince's Trust to start their own small businesses*. The Trust helped two ex-prisoners to start a fishing club; it helped to train lifeguards* on the beaches in Cornwall, and it built a community centre on a poor housing estate*. Since 1976, the Prince's Trust has helped over half a million young people. If you are between 18 and 25 and if you have musical talent, you can go on a one-week music course organised by the Trust. You learn how to set your own music goals, play new styles, play in a band, perform 'live' on the last night of the course, and you get specialist instrument tuition*. It's very popular.

VOCABULARY CHECK LIST
What is it in your language? Find out!

skilful ______
potential ______
in trouble ______
experience ______
disadvantaged ______
small business ______
lifeguard ______
housing estate ______
tuition ______

Who's that girl?

Prince Charles always goes to the Party in the Park and sits with the performers. Who did he sit next to a few years ago? If you guess after one clue, give yourself 10 points. If you guess after two clues, give yourself 9 points, after 3 clues 8 points, etc. Don't cheat! Now make up 10 clues about another famous person. See if your friends can guess who it is.

1 She's a singer.
2 Her birthday is on 21st January.
3 She's a Prince's Trust Ambassador.
4 She used to be in a famous pop group.
5 She's met Nelson Mandela.
6 One of her best friends is married to a world-famous footballer.
7 She's got blonde hair.
8 She's very rich.
9 Her nickname used to be Baby.
10 Her friends' nicknames were Ginger, Sporty, Scary and Posh.

www.princes-trust.org

The Lord Mayor's Show

It takes place on the second Saturday in November every year. Half a million people usually watch the procession* on the streets and three million people watch it on TV. It was the first event* to be broadcast 'live' on television.

During the Show, the new Lord Mayor is taken from the Mansion House in the centre of the City of London, past St Paul's Cathedral built by Sir Christopher Wren, and on to the Law Courts in the Strand. There he makes a promise* to serve the Queen faithfully* for his year as Mayor, and then returns to the Mansion House.

There is always a splendid procession. Four hundred years ago a camel walked in the procession when the Mayor went to meet Queen Elizabeth I. The State Coach (the beautiful golden carriage* carrying the Lord Mayor) is preceded by two hundred soldiers, two hundred horses and sixty-five floats (big lorries with people in carnival costumes). Forty-three tonnes of sand are put on the streets to protect* the horses' feet. There are also sixteen marching bands and eighteen horse-drawn carriages. There are fireworks in the evening. The State Coach was built in 1757, but there has been a Lord Mayor of London (and a Lord Mayor's Show) since 1189. You can read about it in three of Shakespeare's plays, and Canaletto and Hogarth both painted the procession.

The Lord Mayor's Show has only been interrupted* once – for the Duke of Wellington's funeral. To find the date, subtract TOTAL B from TOTAL A:

Add the following numbers:

Bands in the procession	16
Artists who have painted the procession	
Shakespeare's plays which describe it	
Horse-drawn carriages	
The date when the State Coach was built	
Floats in the procession	
Tonnes of sand on the streets of London	
Horses in the procession	
TOTAL A =	

Add the following numbers:

Soldiers in the procession	
The number of weeks in a year	
TOTAL B =	

The year the procession was interrupted for the Duke of Wellington's funeral was ______

VOCABULARY CHECK LIST

What is it in your language? Find out!

- procession
- event
- promise
- faithfully
- carriage
- to protect
- to interrupt

www.lordmayorsshow.org

Legendary Londoners

Dick Whittington

Read these statements about Dick Whittington and match the correct question tags to each one. Look at the alphabet letter in front of each question tag and put it in the space over the correct number in the TAG BOX to find the name of the hill where Dick Whittington heard the church bells.

1 Dick was born in the 1350s, wasn't he?

2 He went to London to find work, ...

3 He didn't have any money, ...

4 Mr Fitzwarren asked Dick to invest* money in a sailing voyage, but Dick wasn't a rich man, ...

5 Dick gave Mr Fitzwarren his cat instead*, and asked him to sell it. Then Dick decided to return to Gloucester, but the church bells started ringing, ...

6 The bells were speaking to him, saying: "Turn again, Whittington!" So Dick turned round and went back to London where he found that Lord Fitzwarren's ship had returned from its voyage. There had been thousands of rats in one of the countries it had visited, ...

7 The brave cat had killed all the rats and the reward* was huge, ... So at last Dick became rich and married Alice Fitzwarren. He was Lord Mayor of London three times and he left all his money to the poor people of London when he died.

8 We all know this story because there is a famous pantomime based on it, ...

TAG BOX

H - didn't he?	**T** - didn't they?
E – isn't there?	~~**H** – wasn't he?~~
G – hadn't there?	**I** – was he?
A – did he?	**G** - wasn't it?

			H				
2	4	7	1	6	3	5	8

Samuel Pepys

Match up the halves of these words and then find where they go in the text about this legendary Londoner. The numbers on each half combine to make a new number between 11 and 21.

Look at the alphabet key and then put the letters in the correct places in the text and they will spell out the name of the street where the Fire of London started.

1 PE	**8 LED**
1 BE	**6 ARY**
2 EXEC	**5 TROYED**
1 RU	**3 ~~TEENTH~~**
1 FAM	**7 EAT**
1 DI	**1 RIAGE**
2 BU	**1 ILT**
1 GR	**0 UTION**
1 MAR	**4 OUS**
1 ~~SEVEN~~	**2 CAME**
1 DES	**9 OPLE**

Alphabet key

11 = D; 12 = N;
~~13 = P;~~ 14 = G;
15 = N; 16 = U;
17 = L; 18 = I;
19 = A; 20 = D;
21 = E

Samuel Pepys was born in the seventeenth (1+3 = P) century. He lived in London and wrote a .... every day. He wrote about life in London, his .... , his friends, the English Civil War* and the .... of King Charles I. After the death of the King, Oliver Cromwell .... England until his own death. Pepys supported* him, but then, like many others, he welcomed the King's son back to England from Holland and he .... the new King Charles. Pepys also wrote about two very .... events* in the life of London: the .... Plague in 1665 which killed thousands of .... and the Fire of London one year later which started in a baker's shop. It .... almost all of the City of London, including St Paul's Cathedral. Sir Christopher Wren .... a new cathedral in the same place.

Sherlock Holmes

Arthur Conan Doyle invented* the character of Sherlock Holmes in 1887. He wrote sixty stories about his famous detective and his friend Dr Watson between 1887 and 1927. He even tried to 'kill' Holmes in 1893, but all the readers protested and he brought him back again in 1901 for a story called *The Hound of the Baskervilles*.

We never learn much about Holmes himself in the stories, except that he was tall, thin, had piercing* eyes and a hawk*-like nose. He played the violin, and was also good at fencing and boxing. He had a passionate interest in chemistry.

Conan Doyle studied medicine in Edinburgh University and this is why Holmes uses forensic* science to solve crimes. Everyone recognises Holmes because of his famous deerstalker hat, his magnifying glass and his pipe. Holmes lived in 221B Baker Street. Some people think he really existed because you can visit Holmes' 'house' which is a museum dedicated to Conan Doyle's hero.

Look at these four groups of objects. Which group comes from 221B Baker Street? Under each group of objects write either:

These can't be from 221B Baker Street because Holmes didn't play ... / smoke ... / wear ... / and didn't like ... OR

These must be from 221B Baker Street because Holmes played ... / smoked ... / wore ... and liked ...

1

....

....

....

....

2

....

....

....

....

3

....

....

....

....

4
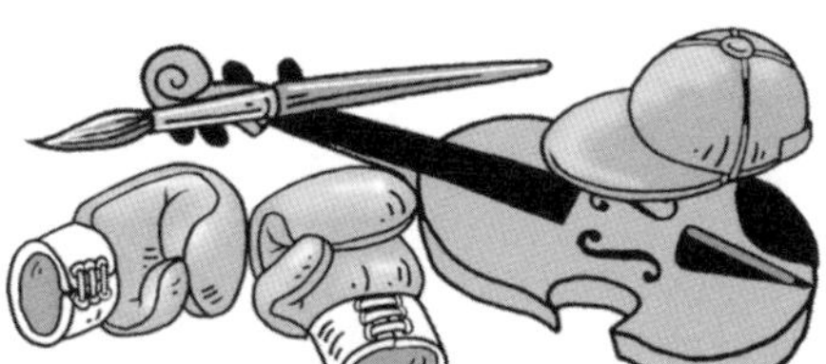

....

....

....

....

VOCABULARY CHECK LIST

What is it in your language? Find out!

to invest

instead

reward

pantomime

civil war

to support

event

to invent

piercing

hawk

forensic

www.longtimeago.com/llta_folktales_dickwhittington.html www.pepys.info/ www.sherlockian.net

Cockney Rhyming Slang

What is a Cockney?

Most people think that a Cockney is anybody who is from or lives in London, but this is not true! Cockney traditionally means a Londoner who lives within five miles of St Mary's Church in Bow, East London.

What is Cockney rhyming slang?

Cockney rhyming* slang is a slang form of language from London.

Most Cockney rhyming slang works by having two words or a phrase. For example: **Daisy Roots** (= boots). The last word in the pair rhymes with its meaning, **Roots = Boots**.

However, to make this more confusing, the rhyming slang is often shortened to the **first word** in the phrase. For example: **Where are my daisies?**

Cockney rhyming slang is confusing for a reason. It was used in the 1800s as a code by East End London street traders* and then also by criminals* who didn't want the police to know what they were talking about. Because the police had to understand this code, they had to write it down, and that is how it became widely known.

Some Cockney rhyming slang is common all over the UK. Here are two examples:

Are you going to rabbit all night!
(Rabbit and pork = talk)

Use your loaf and think next time!
(Loaf of bread = head)

Body parts?

Can you label the parts of the body on this person using Cockney rhyming slang?

1 Hampstead Heath
2 Mince pies
3 Plates of meat
4 Ham and eggs
5 Boat Race

Cockney rhyming slang today

Cockney rhyming slang has recently become fashionable with many young people in the UK, perhaps because it was used in two gangster* movies *Lock Stock and Two Smoking Barrels* and *Snatch*. In fact, many young people have started making up their own modern rhyming slang. It makes them look cool, and like the criminals and street traders before, allows them to talk about things without their parents or teachers understanding.

Modern rhyming slang often uses the names of famous people. Here are three examples. Look at the sentences below. What do you think they mean?

1 Britney Spears
I'm going out for a few *Britneys* at the pub later. Fancy coming?
Meaning = ...

2 Tony Blair
Hey, nice *Tony*. Did you get it cut?
Meaning = ...
....

3 Claire Rayner
(She's a popular agony aunt in the UK – a person who answers people's problems in magazines.)
Wow! You've got new *Claire Rayners*. Are they Adidas?
Meaning = ...
....

www. cockneyrhymingslang.co.uk

VOCABULARY CHECK LIST

What is it in your language? Find out!

to rhyme
trader
criminal
gangster

The British Museum

Put the correct compound adjectives which are missing from the text into the grid to learn the name of one of the most famous exhibits in the British Museum.

well-dressed • multi-coloured • well-read
hand-carved • strange-looking • hard-working
ginger-haired • gold-painted • well-preserved
best-known • unusual-sounding • world-famous

The British Museum is the oldest museum in the world and it covers two million years of world history and culture. Its (1) .... collection of statues, carvings, mummies*, jewels and coins makes it a number one attraction for tourists. It has taken scholars many years to decipher* the (2) .... hieroglyphics (pictures and symbols) on the Egyptian tombs. Amongst the British exhibits from the first century A.D. is Lindow Man, the (3) .... body of a man which was found in a bog*. Lindow Man was poor, unlike the Egyptian mummies which are (4) .... and surrounded by expensive possessions. From Roman Britain there is a wonderful (5) .... mosaic floor; from the twelfth century, the Lewis chess men are probably the Museum's (6) .... items; they are on lots of postcards and you can buy copies of them in the Museum shop. In the African galleries you can see a beautiful (7) .... Nigerian head of a woman. But most people's favourite items are the mummies. The Egyptian queens have (8) .... names such as Seshepenmehit. Their bodies were found in ornate (9) .... coffins deep inside the Pyramids which were built by thousands of (10) .... slaves*. The most famous Egyptian in the British Museum is nicknamed* 'Ginger' because you can still see the original skin and hair on this 5,000-year-old (11) .... farmer whose body was found in the sand along with his burial goods. If you don't like dead bodies, you can visit the Reading Room where some of the world's most (12) .... thinkers, writers and philosophers such as Karl Marx, Ghandi and Dickens used to sit and study.

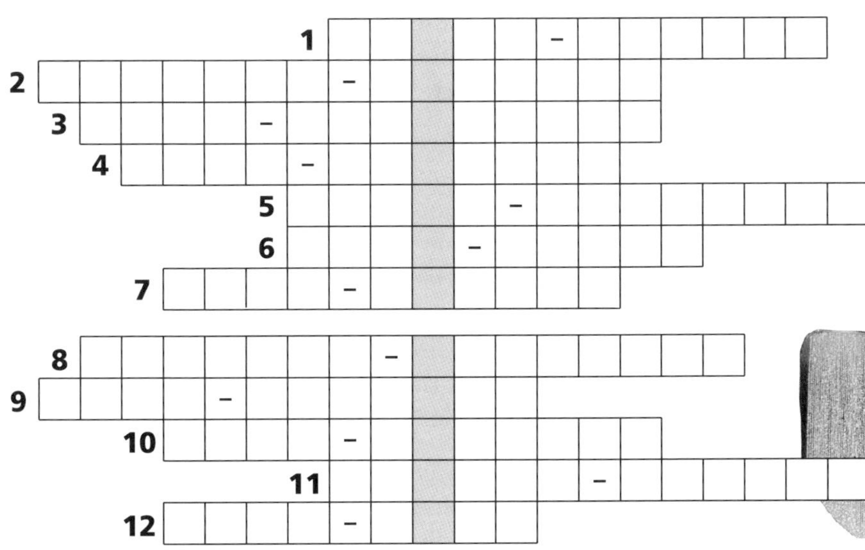

VOCABULARY CHECK LIST
What is it in your language? Find out!

mummy

to decipher

bog

slave

to nickname

The .... is a wonderful treasure from the year 196 B.C. The text in three 'languages' (Hieroglyophics, Demotic and Greek) honours Ptolemy, the Pharaoh at that time. It was discovered in 1799.

www.the britishmuseum.ac.uk

Hampton Court

If you could travel in time and return to the sixteenth century*, you would probably* like to visit Hampton Court Palace which is west of London and on the banks of the River Thames. If you did, you would see that things were very different in those days. You would be surprised how busy the River was, and of course, there were only a few roads and you would only see people on horses or going on foot along them. You would be able to marvel* at the huge parks around the Palace and the deer* walking in them (although you can still see them there today!).

Henry VIII

Thomas Wolsey built the Palace with its 280 guest rooms and he then had to give it to Henry VIII as a present! As a time traveller, you would see long galleries*, beautiful paintings, libraries full of books, a chapel, and 500 servants rushing everywhere preparing meals 'fit for* a king'. Roast deer, roast swan and roast peacock* would probably be on the menu for dinner. You would be able to visit the famous maze* which still exists* today. It's as much fun getting lost in the maze now as it was then.

Henry VIII is famous for having six wives.

Elizabeth I

Elizabeth went to live in Hampton Court Palace one year after she became queen in 1558. She spent Christmas at the Palace and life was wonderful. They all enjoyed banquets, balls, plays, music, dancing, tennis, shooting and hunting. The Great Hall of the Palace is the oldest theatre in England. Explorers* such as Sir Walter Raleigh and Sir Francis Drake were often guests of Elizabeth.

Later Years

The Palace continued to have an interesting history. Sir Christopher Wren built some new parts and both Charles I and Oliver Cromwell lived there. Samuel Pepys was a regular visitor, and rich people went there to escape the Plague in 1665.

If you visited it today, you would be astonished at how magnificent it still looks...but beware of* the ghost of Kathryn Howard!

VOCABULARY CHECK LIST
What is it in your language? Find out!

- century
- probably
- to marvel
- deer
- gallery
- fit for
- peacock
- maze
- to exist
- explorer
- beware of

www.hrp.org.uk/webcode/hampton_home.asp

The Six Wives of Henry VIII

This is the rhyme which we use to remember what happened to Henry's wives:
Divorced, beheaded, died;
Divorced, beheaded, survived.

Read the text and see if you can identify each of the queens.

Anne of Cleves was only married to Henry for a few months.

Neither Katherine Parr nor Anne Boleyn were Henry's first wife.

Jane Seymour died after giving birth to Henry's son, Edward. She wasn't his last wife.

Anne Boleyn and Kathryn Howard were executed.

Catherine of Aragon was married to Henry for twenty-four years.

Kathryn Howard was married to Henry for two years.

1 She married Henry in 1509; she was divorced in 1533.

....

2 She married Henry in 1533; they cut off her head in 1536.

....

3 She married Henry in 1536; she died in 1537.

....

4 She married Henry in 1540; she was divorced in the same year.

Anne of Cleves

5 She married Henry in 1540; they cut her head off in 1542.

....

6 She married Henry in 1543; she died in 1548. (Henry died the year before.)

....

The Maze

Using the same numbers for the six wives as above, which wife would you find if you followed these instructions?

Go to the centre of the maze. Follow the path out and around. When you have to make a choice between left or right, choose right. Follow the path round the corner and she is standing in front of you.

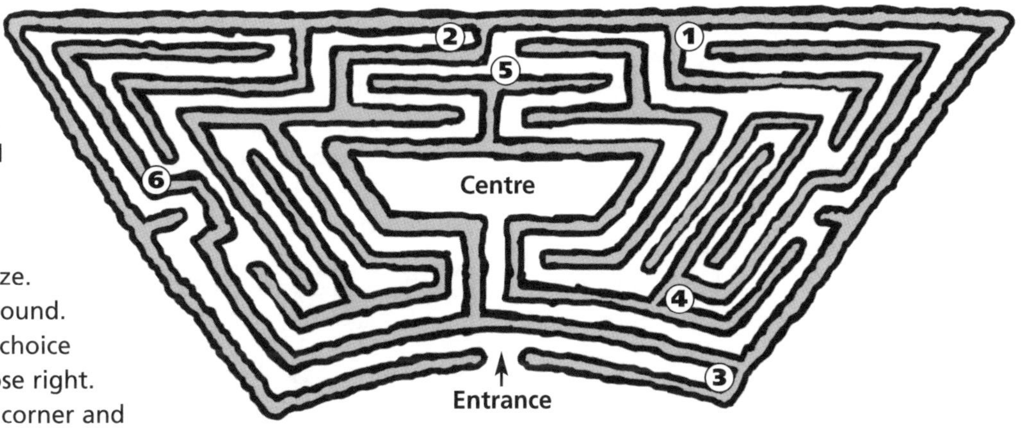

The wife is: ....

Hampton Court Garden

Sir Walter Raleigh brought back lots of presents for Elizabeth. She put two of them in the garden of Hampton Court. Find the names of Henry VIII's six wives in the word search and you will be left with the names of the two plants.

P	C	L	E	V	E	S	O	K
O	F	N	E	O	F	E	K	A
T	N	N	A	T	N	Y	A	T
A	N	H	O	A	B	M	T	H
A	A	O	J	E	O	O	H	E
P	R	W	S	A	L	U	R	R
A	A	A	N	D	E	R	Y	I
R	G	R	T	O	Y	B	N	N
R	O	D	A	C	N	C	O	E
E	N	I	R	E	H	T	A	C

The London Dungeon

The London Dungeon is near London Bridge. It's London's scariest museum. It tells people about London's darker past. Although it's scary*, you can also learn a lot about history, including Boudicca, the Great Plague and Jack the Ripper.

Boudicca

In AD61 thousands of Roman soldiers and their families were living in Britain. Boudicca (sometimes called Boadicea) was queen of the Iceni, an English tribe*. She led the Iceni in a revolt* against the Romans. She was very brave, but her tribe lost the war. The Iceni burned three cities including London.

The Great Plague

In 1665 more than 100,000 people died in the Great Plague*. The disease was carried by fleas* which lived on black rats. The rats came off ships which sailed into London. It wasn't known how the disease was passed from one person to another. At first it was thought that all the dogs and cats in the city were to blame*, so 40,000 dogs and 80,000 cats were destroyed. However, the problem was made worse because the fleas jumped straight from the rats onto people! Rich people were advised to leave London and move to their country houses to avoid* the Plague. One third of all those people left in London died. A red cross was painted on the door of each house where it was known that there was a person dying of the Plague. All the dead bodies were taken and buried in large Plague pits*. Men with carts walked through the streets, and the shouts of "Bring out your dead!" were often heard.

Jack the Ripper

One of London's scariest inhabitants was Jack the Ripper. The streets of London used to be very dangerous in Victorian times because there was a lot of poverty*, homelessness* and crime*, especially in the East End near Whitechapel. Five women were brutally* murdered in ten weeks in 1888 by a man known as 'Jack the Ripper'. 600 policeman tried to solve the crime, but he was never caught. Several famous people were suspected*, including Queen Victoria's son, the Queen's doctor and Walter Sickert, a well-known artist.

VOCABULARY CHECK LIST

What is it in your language? Find out!

scary

tribe

revolt

plague

flea

blame

to avoid

pit

poverty

homelessness

crime

brutally

suspect

www.thedungeons.com

The Prime Suspect

Many theories have been put forward about the identity of Jack the Ripper. Choose the correct verb to complete each sentence below, and join the appropriate dots on the grid. It will spell a word.

1. Patricia Cornwell, the famous American detective writer, **is known** (6 – 9) / **is convinced** ((13 – 15)) that the Ripper was Walter Sickert, the artist.

2. She has even spent her own money on DNA tests which **were carried out** (4 – 5) / **were taken out** (12 – 13) on letters written by the Ripper.

3. Some letters **were sent** (11 – 12) / **were brought** (4 – 7) to the police by the Ripper but others were fakes, written by journalists.

4. One letter **was signed** (3 – 6) / **was chosen** (11 – 13) with the words: "Catch me if you can."

5. The Ripper **was told** (9 – 11) / **was described** (1 – 2) by witnesses as being a short man with a beard who spoke with a foreign accent.

6. Queen Victoria's son, **was inspected** (5 – 8) / **was suspected** (12 –14) of being the Ripper.

7. There was a rumour that he **had been married** (5 – 6) / **has married** (13 –1 6) in secret to a working-class girl in Whitechapel.

8. Some people say that the royal doctor **was persuaded** (8 – 10) / **was given** (2 – 3) to kill the girl's five friends to keep the secret safe.

9. The doctor **had been blessed** (7 – 9) / **had been knighted** (7 – 8) by the Queen, and received the title 'Sir'. His first name was William.

10. People say that he wanted the marriage **to be taken** (5 – 7) / **to be kept** (1 – 4) secret because the girl had had a baby.

11. Jack **was spoken** (3 – 4) **was called** (2 – 5) 'the Ripper' because he ripped (cut) the bodies of his victims.

12. Another suspect was a schoolteacher called Druitt, but his body **was found** (9 – 10) / **was appeared** (1 – 5) in the Thames in December 1888.

13. If the dots below **have been joined** (15 – 16) / **have been left** (11 – 14) correctly, you can see the surname of the royal doctor. You already know his first name and his title.

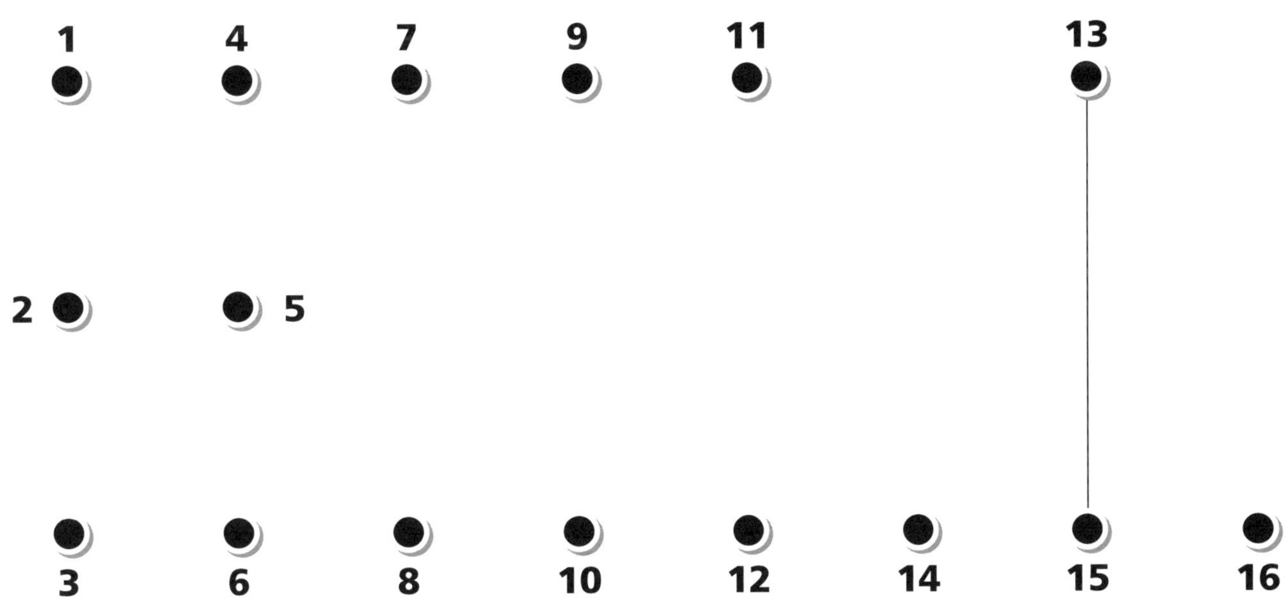

The full name and title of the royal doctor is: ....

Westminster and the Houses of Parliament

The Palace of Westminster, as it used to be called, is one of the oldest buildings in London. It's now the centre of British politics*. Complete the multi-word verbs in the text using words from the list.

at • on • place • out
on • at • ~~about~~ • after
place • on • up • around
down • up • up • around
up • on • away • down

How Did it All Come (1) ....About.... ?

In 1014 the Anglo-Saxons and the Norwegian Vikings sailed (2) .... the River Thames. Danish Vikings stood (3) .... London Bridge and threw spears* and stones (4) .... them, but the Norwegians pulled (5) .... roofs from houses to protect their boats. They used ropes to pull the bridge down. Finally, after many battles, a fierce Danish warrior* called Canute became King of England in 1016. He called (6) .... everyone to live in peace. After he died, King Edward the Confessor carried (7) .... with his good work and built London's first great building*: Westminster Abbey. An earlier church (St Peter's) stood (8) .... the site* before. While the new Abbey was going (9) ...., Edward could look (10) .... it from his home – the Palace of Westminster which was nearby. Sadly, he passed (11) .... a week after the Abbey was finished.

Re-building the Abbey

200 years later, Henry III pulled it (12) .... and built a new abbey. Monks looked (13) .... the farmland around it and grew herbs* (for medicine). You can still go (14) .... the 900-year-old Abbey garden.
Every king or queen since William the Conqueror (1066) has been crowned in the Abbey. The last royal coronation* took (15) .... in 1953. Lots of kings, queens and other famous people are buried there too. When Henry V died, his battle horses were led (16) .... to the altar* with his body. Visitors can walk (17) .... the Abbey when there are no church services and can see the memorials put (18) .... to people like Shakespeare and Chaucer.

The Houses of Parliament

Royal Christmas feasts*, coronation banquets and trials* have taken (19) .... in Westminster Hall which is the oldest part of the palace still remaining. In 1834 a terrible fire wiped (20) .... a lot of the old palace. It was rebuilt, and contains 1,000 rooms. It contains the House of Commons (the main parliament) and the House of Lords where people with noble titles (*Lord, Lady, Sir*, etc) discuss laws suggested by Members of Parliament in the House of Commons.

VOCABULARY CHECK LIST
What is it in your language? Find out!

- politics ....
- spear ....
- warrior ....
- building ....
- site ....
- herbs ....
- coronation ....
- altar ....
- feast ....
- trial ....

www.bonfirenight.net/index.php

Guy Fawkes and the Gunpowder Plot

Guy Fawkes was one of the group of men who plotted to blow up the Houses of Parliament in 1605. The Roman Catholic plotters wanted the Protestant King James to be more tolerant to Catholics. One plotter sent a letter to warn a friend not to go the Houses of Parliament. The King found out and his guards searched the cellars of Parliament and found Guy Fawkes.

Go through the maze joining up the multi-word verbs which complete the sentences. If you join them up correctly and take the alphabet letters in the corners of the squares you will see the name of the leader of the plotters.

It was late at night when Guy Fawkes .... to the cellars of the Houses of Parliament. He looked round for somewhere to sit. At first he .... on one of the barrels, but then he felt tired so he .... on the floor. He fell asleep for a few minutes but .... when he heard a noise. He .... quickly and hid behind a barrel. A voice .... "Who's there?!". Suddenly a group of guards .... and .... one of the barrels. They .... the corner and saw something move. Guy almost .... as he tried to .... but they .... him and caught him. He was .... , tortured and executed and a few days later all the other plotters were caught and killed too. Now English people burn a 'guy' on a bonfire each November 5th to remind everyone of that moment in history.

START

went down **R**	sat down **O**	lay down **B**	lay in **S**	put on **E**
got by **A**	got up **R**	woke up **E**	fell off **C**	sat up **U**
passed out **V**	called out **T**	called on **H**	came up **F**	carried away **Y**
gave up **M**	burst in **C**	knocked over **A**	came round **T**	ran after **B**
came across **L**	broke down **I**	brought up **P**	fell over **E**	run away **S**

London Parks

London has more parks and big gardens than almost any other capital city. Put the correct missing words in the sentences and then put the words into the trees and you can find the name of the London park which has an open air theatre. During the summer you can watch Shakespeare's plays when it isn't raining.

Hyde Park

Hyde Park is the **1** ......largest...... central London Park. It used to be a royal hunting forest and sometimes **2** .... used to go there to **3** .... duels*. There's a big lake in the middle of Hyde Park called the Serpentine. Some people swim in the Serpentine on Christmas Day.

Kensington Gardens

Part of the lake is in Kensington Gardens. **4** ...., wild bulls* and wild boar* used to live there a long time ago. Speakers' Corner is in Hyde Park near Marble Arch. It's a place where **5** .... can go to make a speech on a Sunday afternoon. There's a **6** .... of Peter Pan in the park and also a tree full of carved* elves* called The Elfin Oak.

St James's Park

There is an old French game called *paille maille*. It's like croquet* and Charles II used to play this game in St James's Park. The road next to it is now called Pall Mall.

Regent's Park

Regent's Park also used to be a hunting forest. Over one hundred **7** .... ago people used to **8** .... things on canals. You can still hire boats on the Regent's Canal and sail to Camden in north London. And of course there's the Zoo in Regent's Park where people used to visit Guy the gorilla.

Holland Park

Holland Park is a pretty little park near Notting Hill and it's full of bluebells* in spring time.

Richmond Park

King **9** .... the First used to enjoy hunting and he made Richmond an enclosed* park in 1632. It's one of the largest enclosed parks in **10** .... There are 600 deer in this huge **11** ...., and ducks and swans on the ponds. 600,000 years ago lions and rhinoceroses used to live there.

statue	park
years	Britain
people	Charles
anyone	wolves
fight	~~largest~~
transport	

VOCABULARY CHECK LIST

What is it in your language? Find out!

- duel
- bull
- boar
- carved
- elves
- croquet
- bluebell
- enclosed

Tree 1 Tree 2

www.royalparks.gov.uk

Art in London

Pick the correct passive verbs in the text to discover what has made the ten British artists on the bottom half of this page famous.

Tate Modern

Most people **1** ...are very impressed... *are very interested* **(j)** / *are very impressed* **(f)** by the amount of art on display in London. The National Gallery in Trafalgar Square has one of the largest collections of pictures in the world. Paintings by Da Vinci, Titian, Velasquez, Holbein and many others **2** .... *are exhibited* **(c)** / *are extended* **(a)** there. The National Portrait Gallery **3** .... *has found itself* **(i)** / *is situated* **(a)** just around the corner from the National Gallery. Tate Britain is on the River Thames and it's near the Houses of Parliament. There are a lot of modern paintings there as well as pictures by Turner and Constable, but many of the very recent ones **4** .... *have been borrowed* **(j)** / *have been taken* **(g)** to Tate Modern. Tate Modern used to be a power station with a gigantic turbine* hall which is now a gallery, and it's **5** .... *linked* **(h)** / *lined* **(b)** to St Paul's Cathedral by a bridge **6** .... *called* **(c)** / *known* **(b)** as 'The Wobbly* Bridge' because it used to move when a lot of people walked on it. Tate Modern **7** .... *was engineered* **(d)** / *was designed* **(e)** by Giles Gilbert Scott who was also the architect responsible for* Liverpool's new cathedral and London's red telephone boxes. Art enthusiasts **8** .... *are transported* **(d)** / *are translated* **(j)** from Tate Modern to Tate Britain by a boat service called 'Tate to Tate'. In Tate Modern you can see paintings by modern artists such as Andy Warhol, Picasso and Lichtenstein and 'op art' (optical illusions) by Bridget Riley.

1. **Stubbs** (1724-1806) is best known for
2. **Constable** (1776-1837) is best known for
3. **Turner** (1775-1851) is best known for
4. **Blake** (1757-18270 is best known for
5. **Hogarth** (1697-1764) is best known for
6. **Gainsborough** (1727-1788) is best known for
7. **David Hockney** (1937-) is best known for
8. **Lowry** (1887-1976) is best known for

a) his paintings of sea, sky, ships and landscapes

b) his paintings of ladies in big long dresses with large curly silver wigs

c) his paintings of English country landscapes

d) his paintings of British northern industrial towns full of 'matchstick* men'

e) his paintings of Californian swimming pools and 1960s people

f) his paintings of horses

g) his mystical* religious paintings

h) his satirical* drawings of 18th century London life

VOCABULARY CHECK LIST

What is it in your language? Find out!

turbine

wobbly

responsible for

matchstick

mystical

satirical

www.nationalgallery.org.uk

Pubs and Clubs

Many of the pubs in London have been there for hundreds of years. The 'club scene' is more recent. You can dance to all kinds of music: garage, techno, hip hop and rock. Many of the clubs have age limits* and rules about how you are allowed to dress.

You are not allowed to buy an alcoholic drink in a pub if you are under eighteen. Recently* the laws have changed and some pubs are allowed to serve drinks all day. Before the pubs close, the landlord* shouts, "Last orders!" and people are allowed to buy one more drink before the pub closes. You aren't allowed to take children into a pub unless the pub has a restaurant. Some pubs have beer gardens and families are allowed to sit outside. People enjoy sitting round a table with a drink telling jokes and clever stories like this one. Put the correct verbs into the spaces.

agreed
fell
stood
was
smiled
poured
came
began
lost
shook

A philosophy professor (1) .... before his class and (2) .... filling a large glass jar with rocks. The students (3) .... that the jar (4) .... full. So the professor (5) .... and picked up a box of small pebbles and poured them into the jar. The pebbles, of course, (6) .... into the small spaces. Then the professor (7) .... a box of sand into the jar, (8) .... it, and the sand completely filled the jar.*

"This jar represents your life," said the professor. "The rocks are the important things – your family, your health; if you (9) .... everything else, your life would still be full. The pebbles are the smaller things that matter – your job, your house, your car. The sand represents the trivial things. If you put the sand into the jar first, there is no room for the pebbles or the rocks, just like life. Take care of the rocks first – the things that really matter. The rest is just sand."*

Then a student (10) .... to the front of the class and poured a can of beer into the jar and it was easily absorbed. The moral of this tale is: No matter how full your life is, there is always room for beer.*

VOCABULARY CHECK LIST
What is it in your language? Find out!

limit ________

recently ________

landlord ________

pebble ________

trivial ________

to absorb ________

www.pubs.com

Greenwich

The best way to visit Greenwich is to go by boat from Westminster pier. Greenwich is the home of the National Maritime Museum and the Royal Observatory.

The National Maritime Museum (designed by Sir Christopher Wren) has got a big collection of maps, manuscripts, models of famous ships and portraits of famous sailors and explorers.

The Royal Observatory was built in 1678 to solve the problem of finding longitude – a ship's exact position east and west while at sea and out of sight of land. Early sailors used the stars to help them navigate and they could tell the time from the position of the sun. However, they needed to know what the time was at a fixed reference point* because time moves forwards and backwards every 15° one travels (east or west). Clocks were not accurate* at sea, and each country had its own zero meridian*. In 1884, at a conference in Washington, USA, most countries in the world agreed to make Greenwich the source* of the prime* meridian (0°).

You can also find out about the night sky at the planetarium in Greenwich.

Put the times on the clocks and use the semaphore code to find out a fact about a very cold planet.

1 **a)** nine o'clock; **b)** ten past eight; **c)** five past eleven; **d)** eleven o'clock **e)** ten to nine

a b c d e

2 **a)** five to three; **b)** five past six; **c)** twenty to seven; **d)** quarter past nine; **e)** twenty past nine

a b c d e

3 **a)** twenty past nine; **b)** five past eleven; **c)** twenty-five to five

a b c

1 ◯◯◯◯◯ takes 248 **2** ◯◯◯◯◯ to go round the **3** ◯◯◯

VOCABULARY CHECK LIST

What is it in your language? Find out!

reference point

accurate

meridian

source

prime

www.rog.nmm.ac.uk

Charles Dickens

Charles Dickens was born in Portsmouth in 1812 and died in London in 1870. He is buried in Poets' Corner in Westminster Abbey.

Victorian London

Dickens spent most of his life in London and often used to walk between ten and twenty miles* all over the city when he was unable to sleep and was thinking about the plot of a new novel. While walking, he used to observe the sights, sounds and smells of London in order to write about them. In 1800 there were one million people in London, but by 1880 there were four and a half million! Because of the Industrial Revolution, Britain, and especially London, grew very quickly.

People used to travel through the streets of London in horse-drawn carriages. Every hour at least one thousand carriages crossed London Bridge, so there used to be a lot of mess* on the streets from the horses!

It also used to be a noisy city because people who were selling things used to shout to advertise their goods. People used to drink water from the Thames so it's not surprising that many of them used to get very ill and many people died of cholera. The city used to smell and it was also very dirty. Smoke used to pour from the chimneys of thousands of houses and factories; the streets were dark because there only used to be gas lamps, and the dark alleys* were full of beggars*, thieves* and people who were drunk.

Poverty

London used to be a terrible place for poor people, especially children. In 1839 nearly half of all the funerals* in London were for children under the age of ten. Those who survived had little or no education and Dickens believed that education was the way to break the cycle of poverty as it had done for him. In his books he used to expose all these awful social* problems.

VOCABULARY CHECK LIST

What is it in your language? Find out!

mile ______

mess ______

alley ______

beggar ______

thief ______

funeral ______

social ______

installment ______

soap opera ______

www.fidnet.com/~dap1955/

www.dickens/dickens'_london_map.html

Dickens' novels

Dickens used to publish all his stories in serialised form. People used to read weekly installments* of his novels in magazines and he became a publishing phenomenon. Each installment used to end with a 'cliff-hanger' – a dramatic moment which left everyone desperate to know what happened next, just like today's modern soap operas*. Dickens said: "I make them laugh; I make them cry; I make them wait." Solve the clues below, write them in the grid, and you will see the name of all Dickens' novels. In the shaded squares you will also see the name of one of his most famous characters. When you see CAPITAL LETTERS, just copy them into the grid.

A number between 1 and 3 (P4)
Shared by two or more people (H2)
Miserable, gloomy (B1)
A place where you buy things (K4)
An organ which takes poison from the body (A2)
English name for the Christmas saint (J1)
You use a timetable to find the – of trains (G2)
A reddish-brown coloured metal (N2)
To think something is going to arrive (O2)
A verb often confused with *make* (M2)
Farm building where cows live (D1)
Preposition meaning *near* or *next to* (D3)
A girl's name and Christmas song (L3)
A meadow where cows live (N3)
Preposition meaning *near* or *next to* (J3)
Pages of a book are made from it (I3)
Fibre or cord in a candle which burns (I2)
A conjunction, eg fish – chips (C3)
A fascinating object or desire to know things (K3)
A big December holiday (L2)
Where people live (B2)
Opposite of *soft* (G1)

Definite article (K1)
Indefinite article (P1)
Humour (F4)
Short for *Edward* (E1)
Large towns (P5)
A pal (H3)
I (O4)
OOD (E4)
S (O6)
Opposite of *new* (K2)
Short for *Doctor* (E3)
A cheap metal (F2)
Story (P2)
MAR (F1)
Opposite of *lose* (E2)
MBEY (C2)
A cup – tea (P3)
Indefinite article (L1)

Very big (O1)
Opposite of *big* (M1)
RUDGE (D4)
Mother, father, daughter – (C4)
O (A1)
To turn (A3)
How do you – ? (C1)
A (D2)
CHUZZLE (F3)
I get up – seven o'clock (O3)
I sleep late – Sundays (O5)
DAVID (N1)
RRIT (M3)
NICKLE (J2)
Belonging to us (H1)
To take or choose (I1)
S (I4)

The famous Dickens character is:

....

Answers

Pages 8 & 9

Arriving in London

1 **1** Heathrow, **2** Gatwick, **3** Luton, **4** Stansted, **5** City
2 You go to passport control
3 You go to baggage reclaim
4

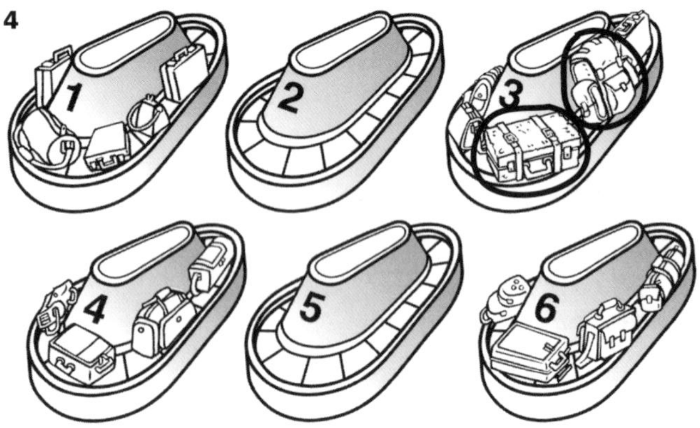

5 You go to the Exit

6

Name of airport	Where do you arrive?	How long does it take?	How much does it cost?
Heathrow	Paddington	15 mins	£13
Gatwick	Victoria	30 mins	£11
Stansted	Liverpool Street	45 mins	£13
Luton	London Bridge	30 mins	£10

Pages 10 & 11

London transport

Help the tourist!

1 = bus 1 e, **2** = bus 88 c, **3** = bus 42 d, **4** = bus 159 b, **5** = bus 11 a

Travelcard

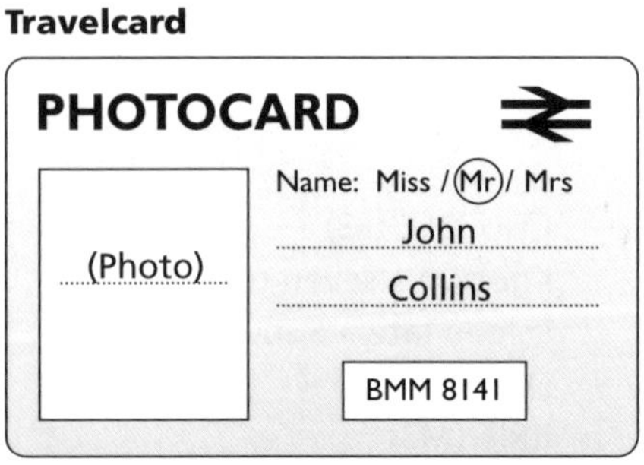

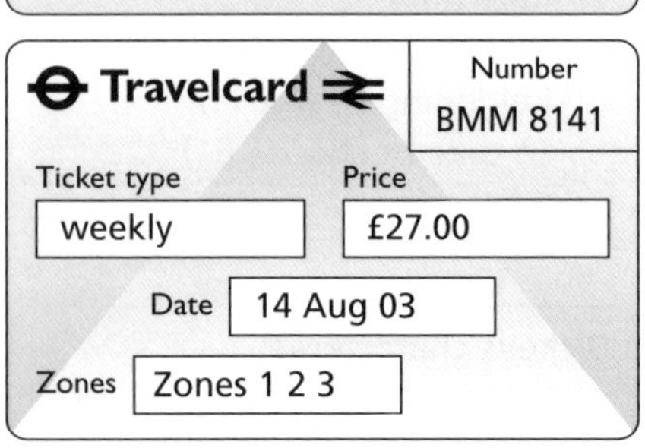

Buying a travel card / ticket.

Tourist: A one-day travelcard to London, **please**.
(**Not** please a one-day travelcard)
Travel assistant: That's £4.90 **please**.
Tourist: Here's £5.00.
Travel assistant: Thank you. Here's your ticket and change.
Tourist: Thank you.

Pages 12 & 13

Going by Tube

1 – Central, **2** – Circle, **3** – Piccadilly, **4** – Victoria, **5** – Northern, **6** – District, **7** – Bakerloo, **8** – Hammersmith and City, **9** – Jubilee, **10** – Metropolitan, **11** – Waterloo and City, **12** – Docklands Light Railway

Finish these sentences:

a three, **b** Paddington and Notting Hill Gate, **c** Piccadilly

Pages 14 & 15

The London Eye

A great view!

1 Trafalgar Square, **2** Tower Bridge, **3** Big Ben, **4** St Paul's Cathedral, **5** A black taxi

How much does it cost?

1 £16.50, **2** £100.00, **3** £20.00, **4** £22.00, **5** £40.00

Pages 16 & 17

The Tower of London

Numbers search

A = three hundred (in the Crown Jewels paragraph)
B = seven (in the ravens paragraph)
C = nine hundred (in the introduction)
D = forty (in the Beefeaters paragraph)

Escape from the Tower

Pages 18 & 19

The River Thames

Frogtours

1 e, **2** f, **3** g, **4** d, **5** i, **6** b, **7** c, **8** a, **9** h

Pages 20 & 21

London Football Clubs

Which player?

1 = David James; **2** = David James; **3** = David James; **4** = Hernan Crespo

Mascots

1 b, **2** d, **3** c, **4** a

Football chants:

1 = Chelsea; **2** = Tottenham; **3** = West Ham

Pages 22 & 23

Madame Tussaud's

1 George Bush, **2** Kylie Minogue, **3** David Beckham, **4** Jennifer Lopez

In the modelling room

1 It's the Queen's hair. **2** It's James Bond's arm. **3** It's Charlie Chaplin's moustache. **4** They're Marilyn Monroe's legs.

Page 24

Buckingham Palace

1 c, **2** a, **3** e, **4** b, **5** d, **6** g, **7** f

Page 25

The London Butterfly House

Find the butterflies

1 b, **2** f, **3** c, **4** e, **5** d, **6** a

Pages 26 & 27

Hamleys

Which floor?

1 fifth floor, **2** basement, **3** first floor, **4** third floor, **5** second floor

Speaking

1 basement, **2** second floor, **3** first floor, **4** first floor, **5** ground floor and third floor, **6** the ground floor and the fifth floor

Pages 28 & 29

Harrods

Rules of the shop

1 can't, **2** can't, **3** can, **4** can't, **5** can, **6** can't

Problems, problems

1 It's too big.
2 They are too short.
3 My mother already has one of these.
4 It's got a hole in it.
5 It's broken (The zip is broken).

Take it back

Shop Assistant: Can I help you?
Customer: Yes, it's this jumper.
Shop Assistant: OK. What's the problem with it?
Customer: It's too big
Shop Assistant: Would you like an exchange or refund?
Customer: I'd like an exchange. I'd like this jumper in a smaller size.
Shop Assistant: That's fine. Have you got the receipt?
Customer: Yes, here it is.

Pages 30 & 31

London's Markets

1 d, **2** e, **3** a, **4** b, **5** c

At the market

1 is £10.00, **2** is £25.00, **3** are £1.50, **4** are £0.30, **5** is £60.00, **6** are £20.00

Pages 32 & 33

London's Theatreland

London musicals

1 d, **2** a, **3** b, **4** g, **5** f, **6** c, **7** e

Booking a ticket

1 a, **2** b, **3** a, **4** b, **5** b, **6** a, **7** a

Pages 34 & 35

Dogs in London

Spot the dog

1 b, **2** c, **3** a

Pet Quiz!

1 c, **2** b, **3** c, **4** a, **5** c, **6** b

Where's Sam?

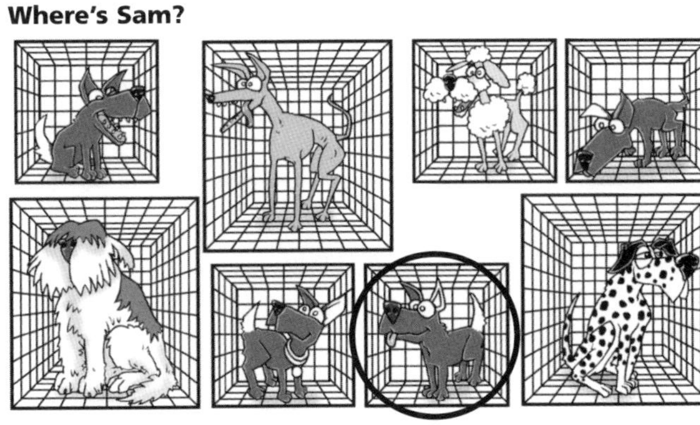

Pages 36 & 37

Eating out: Food in London

Food dishes

1 fish and chips, **2** noodles, **3** curry, **4** cheeseburger, **5** pizza, **6** sushi

Fish and chips: "Open or wrapped?"

If you say 'open' you can eat your chips immediately. If you say 'wrapped'. They will put your chips in paper to keep them warm so you can eat them at home.

Restaurant names

1 Planet Hollywood = American,
2 Masala Zone = Indian,
3 Yo! Sushi = Japanese,
4 Pizza Express = Italian,
5 Wok Wok = Chinese,
6 The Chippy = English
7 Café Rouge = French,
8 Noodle Time = Chinese

At the restaurant

The dish is traditional fish and chips with vinegar.

Who says it?

Ready to order? (W)
I'm a vegetarian. (C)
I'm allergic to nuts. (C)
Would you like some pepper? (W)
Would you like anything to drink? (W)
Table for two please. (C)
I'd like to pay please. (C)
Where would you like to sit? (W)
Can I have another fork? (C)
I'd like the green salad. (C)

Pages 38 & 39

Everyday Londoners

Writing home: suggested answers

Dear ***Mum / Dad***
How are you? I arrived in London on Tuesday.
I'm living in ***a bedsit*** *in* ***Clapham / Kensington.***
The most difficult thing about living in London ***is finding a place to live and understanding the transport system.***
The best thing about living in London is ***the nightlife.***
Hope you are all well.
I will call you next week.
Love ***Anna.***

Calling for a job

Gianni is too casual and chatty.
1 = c, **2** = d, **3** = a, **4** = e, **5** = b

Suggested answers for Mr Briggs

Yes, speaking. How can I help?
Yes, we're still looking for people.
Yes, of course. It's a part-time job. We are looking for somebody who can work evenings from 5pm -11pm, six days a week. It's £5.50 an hour. Have you got any experience of waiting?
That sounds great. We're having interviews this Tuesday at 3pm. Would you like to come?

Pages 40 & 41

The Boat Race

Boat Race statistics

1 fastest,
2 heaviest,
3 lightest,
4 youngest,
5 smallest,
6 tallest,
7 woman,
8 first,
9 female.

F	A	S	T	E	S	T	L	T
E	A	N	S	D	S	S	I	S
M	Y	P	E	E	R	E	G	E
A	O	B	L	E	R	G	H	I
L	T	L	L	●	●	N	T	V
E	A	S	A	A	N	U	E	A
T	N	A	M	O	W	O	S	E
F	I	R	S	T	K	Y	T	H

The oldest person to take part in the Boat Race was ANDY PROBERT who was 38. He was the Cambridge cox in 1992. In 1912 both boats SANK

Pages 42 & 43

Wimbledon: The Home of Tennis

Wimbledon rules

1 must, **2** mustn't, **3** must, **4** mustn't, **5** mustn't

Tennis talk

1 a, **2** b, **3** a

Pages 44 & 45

Theme Parks Around London

The Tomb Blaster Puzzle

The correct choices spell the words: *The Forbidden Kingdom.*

Five stars

extreme – five stars, intense – four stars, thrilling – three stars, fun for the family – two stars; for little children – one star.

Page 47

The London Aquarium

The correct choices spell out the sentence: *More people in the U.S. are killed by bees than sharks.*

Pages 48 & 49

London Zoo

The zoo maze

couldn't , transferred, arrived, walked, doubled, poked, died, opened, bit, ate, hurried, came, took, bred.
The okapi are also known by the popular name of jungle giraffes

Pages 50 & 51

EastEnders

1 e, **2** c, **3** g, **4** d, **5** a, **6** h, **7** f, **8** b, **9** i

Pages 52 & 53

The London Marathon

True or false?

2 False. **3** False. You have to be over 18. **4** True. **5** False. People collecting money for charity run in costumes. **6** True.

Pages 54 & 55

Notting Hill and the Carnival

Party people

1 = She's going to win the costume competition.
2 = He's going to be sick.
3 = She's going to have a headache.
4 = He's going to steal the mobile phone.
5 = He's going to get sunburn.

Notting Hill Carnival Route
The carnival is on August the 23rd. The date of the carnival can vary from year to year, but is always on the bank holiday weekend at the end of August.

Page 56
Leicester Square: London Cinemas
Film certificates
U – c, PG – e, 12A – d, 15 – a, 18 – b.
The correct answers in the film star puzzle spell out the name of the film: *Love Actually*.

Page 57
Music in London
The missing words are:
1 strong, **2** heart, **3** feed, **4** impossible, **5** man, **6** dream, **7** maybe, **8** at, **9** with, **10** you, **11** saves, **12** I'll.
The name of the concert venue is WEMBLEY ARENA.

Page 58
Party in the Park
Who's that girl?
The mystery person sitting next to Prince Charles is Emma Bunton who used to sing with the Spice Girls.

Page 59
The Lord Mayor's Show
The correct figures in the maths problem are:
(Total A): 16, 2, 3, 18, 1757, 65, 43, 200 = 2104.
(Total B): 200, 52 = 252. Total A minus Total B = 1852, the year of the Duke of Wellington's funeral.

Pages 60 & 61
Legendary Londoners
Dick Whittington:
The correct choices spell HIGHGATE. This is a region in the north of London, near Hampstead Heath.

Samuel Pepys:
The correct missing words are: seventeenth, diary, marriage, execution, ruled, became, famous, great, people, destroyed, built. The letters in the grid therefore spell out the name: PUDDING LANE.

Sherlock Holmes:
1 These can't be from 221B Baker Street because Holmes didn't play tennis.
2 These can't be from 221B Baker Street because Holmes didn't play the trumpet.
3 These must be from 221B Baker Street because Holmes played the violin, wore a deer stalker hat, used a magnifying glass, was a fencer and liked chemistry.
4 These can't be from 221B Baker Street because Holmes didn't wear a baseball cap, he didn't like painting and he didn't play football.

Page 62
Cockney Rhyming Slang
Body parts
1 Hampstead Heath = teeth
2 Mince pies = eyes
3 Plates of meat = feet
4 Ham and eggs = legs
5 Boat Race = face

Modern rhyming slang
1 Britney Spears = beers
2 Tony Blair = hair
3 Claire Rayners = trainers

Page 63
The British Museum
1 world-famous,
2 strange-looking,
3 well-preserved,
4 well-dressed,
5 multi-coloured,
6 best-known,
7 hand-carved,
8 unusual-sounding,
9 gold-plated,
10 hard-working,
11 ginger-haired,
12 well-read.
The shaded letters therefore spell 'Rosetta Stone'.

Pages 64 & 65
Hampton Court
The Six Wives of Henry VIII
1 Catherine of Aragon;
2 Anne Boleyn;
3 Jane Seymour;
4 Anne of Cleves;
5 Kathryn Howard;
6 Katherine Parr.

The Maze
The wife you would meet in the maze is Catherine of Aragon, wife number 1.

Hampton Court Garden
The wordsearch answers are:

P	C	L	E	V	E	S	O	K
O	F	N	E	O	F	E	K	A
T	N	N	A	T	N	Y	A	T
A	N	H	O	A	B	M	T	H
A	A	O	J	E	O	O	H	E
P	R	W	S	A	L	U	R	R
A	A	A	N	D	E	R	Y	I
R	G	R	T	O	Y	B	N	N
R	O	D	A	C	N	C	O	E
E	N	I	R	E	H	T	A	C

The remaining letters spell the words: POTATOES AND TOBACCO.

Pages 66 & 67

The London Dungeon

The prime suspect

1 is convinced;
2 were carried out;
3 were sent;
4 was signed;
5 was described;
6 was suspected;
7 had been married;
8 was persuaded;
9 had been knighted;
10 to be kept;
11 was called;
12 was found;
13 have been joined.

When all the dots have been joined correctly, they spell out the word: **gull**. Sir William Gull was the name of the royal doctor who was a possible suspect in the Ripper murders. It is said that he was covering up for the Queen's son.

Page 68

Westminster and the Houses of Parliament

1 about; **2** up; **3** on; **4** at; **5** down; **6** on; **7** on; **8** on; **9** up; **10** at; **11** away; **12** down; **13** after; **14** around; **15** place; **16** up; **17** around; **18** up; **19** place; **20** out.

Page 69

Guy Fawkes and the Gunpowder Plot

The correct choices of verb spell out the name Robert Catesby

Page 70

London Parks

Tree 1

1 L A R G E S T
2 P E O P L E
3 F I G H T
4 W O L V E S
5 A N Y O N E
6 S T A T U E
7 Y E A R S

Tree 2

8 T R A N S P O R T
9 C H A R L E S
10 B R I T A I N
11 P A R K

Page 71

Art in London

1 f, **2** c, **3** a, **4** g, **5** h, **6** b, **7** e, **8** d

Page 72

Pubs and Clubs

1 stood, **2** began, **3** agreed, **4** was, **5** smiled, **6** fell, **7** poured, **8** shook, **9** lost, **10** came.

Page 73

Greenwich

Pluto takes 248 years to go round the Sun.

Pages 74 & 75

Charles Dickens

A [1]O [2]L I V E R ■ [3]T W I S T
B [1]B L E A K ■ [2]H O U S E
C [1]D O [2]M B E Y ■ [3]A N D ■ [4]S O N
D [1]B A R N [2]A [3]B Y ■ [4]R U D G E
E [1]E D [2]W I N ■ [3]D R [4]O O D
F [1]M A R [2]T I N ■ [3]C H U Z Z L E [4]W I T
G [1]H A R D ■ [2]T I M E S
H [1]O U R ■ [2]M U T U A L ■ [3]F R I E N D
I [1]P I C K [2]W I C K ■ [3]P A P E R [4]S
J [1]N I C H O L A S ■ [2]N I C K L E [3]B Y
K [1]T H E ■ [2]O L D ■ [3]C U R I O S I T Y ■ [4]S H O P
L [1]A ■ [2]C H R I S T M A S ■ [3]C A R O L
M [1]L I T T L E ■ [2]D O [3]R R I T
N [1]D A V I D ■ [2]C O P P E R [3]F I E L D
O [1]G R E A T ■ [2]E X P E C T [3]A T [4]I [5]O N [6]S
P [1]A ■ [2]T A L E ■ [3]O F ■ [4]T W O ■ [5]C I T I E S

Dickens' Novels

The famous character is Ebenezer Scrooge (from A Christmas Carol)